# The
# Grass-Roots
# Mind in
# America

# The Grass-Roots Mind in America

## The American Sense of Absolutes

## by Conal Furay

**New Viewpoints**
A Division of Franklin Watts
New York | London | 1977

Library of Congress Cataloging in Publication
Data

Furay, Conal.
   The grass-roots mind in America.

   Bibliography: p.
   Includes index.
   1. United States—Civilization—1970–
   2. National characteristics, American.   I. Title.
   E169.F96 1977      973      76–48927
   ISBN 0–531–05391–1
   ISBN 0–531–05598–1 pbk.

New Viewpoints
A Division of Franklin Watts
730 Fifth Avenue
New York, New York 10019

To my sister Alice, for a special reason,
and to my wife Jean, for all kinds of reasons

# PREFACE

There is a great story in Jerome Bruner's *The Process of Education* about a teacher who set out to explain a theory to a group of students. When finished he found little but puzzlement mirrored on their faces. So, laboriously, he repeated his remarks, only to find the same blank looks. Exasperated, the teacher explained the essentials of the theory a third time, and finally, said he later, "Finally, *I* understood it." This story reflects the origin of this book. In teaching American intellectual history, I have been frequently asked by students why the course deals with all the isms and abstractions that have bored the common man—then and now—and fails to explore the ideas and attitudes that really do occupy his mind. So, easily at first, then laboriously, I explained the vital distinction between a society's men of ideas and those for whom abstract ideas are secondary. And finally, the third time I explained it, or more likely the tenth time, *I* understood it.

This is a book based upon that distinction. It is an attempt to explore that mind—to be called here the "grass-roots" mind—which is not written about in American intellectual histories, perhaps because its orientation is not toward ideas but toward concrete realities and ways to deal with them. This is not to say that ideas (and ideals) are of no importance to this mind, only that such abstractions bump against the priorities of concrete life and fixed principle and are most often fended off. The cardinal principle of the grass-roots mind is that "the concrete precedes the abstract"; its tendency is to return to familiar thoughts and images rather than to venture into new symbolic worlds; its logic is more often rooted in intuition and emotional attachment than in rational analysis; it seeks a world of social thickness that can provide insulation against the shocks of too much reality. Out of all this emerges a coherent pattern of thought, but, because it is prosaic, it is not the kind of pattern that has attracted historians of thought. They are more interested in the major traffic in ideas of a society.

Still, in the twentieth century the grass-roots mind has begun to get its due, as social historians have explored the folklore, popular culture, and social patterns of the American common man. This book is a continuation of those efforts, its primary purpose being to get a wide-angle picture of the American multitude, and thus to identify its main features. The main features of the picture I took are summarized in Chapter One. The other chapters provide a look at those forms of life that have been and continue to be important in this country, including, in order, popular culture, the small-town ethos, and a variety of social "retreats" that deeply influence large numbers of Americans. What emerged from the study as a whole was the inescapable conclusion that grass-roots America clings to cultural patterns sometimes associated with an earlier day. In this American mentality is rooted a powerful cultural continuity that seems to defy the forces of change so continuously set before our eyes in academic literature and in the media.

Any historian or writer left to his own resources must quickly go bankrupt, and I am no exception. This is my way of entering into the subject of my debts to others for their help in this undertaking. Deserving of first mention are the many scholars whose works I have consulted in my research. At the personal level I want to express my gratitude to Professor R. Lynn Kelley of

Webster College, a fine political scientist and a good friend. He read the entire manuscript, flooring me for the count at several points (though with a velvet glove); but the major changes that resulted from the knockdowns have materially improved the final product. Equally important have been the suggestions of Carole Fitzgerald Hayes of Chicago, Illinois, whose gift for words exceeds that of anyone else I know. Will Davison of New Viewpoints and Elaine Chubb have earned my gratitude several times over by the exacting critiques they gave my basic manuscript. Further back, as a graduate student in educational psychology twenty years ago at Creighton University, I much admired the perspectives of Professor Leo R. Kennedy; without knowing it he has deeply influenced my professional career and continues to do so through the present work. I am also indebted to the Webster College Board of Directors for its graciousness in granting me a sabbatical for professional development, and to the faculty members of the History and Political Science Department for their generous words and moral support. The staff of the Eden-Webster Library gave me assistance at every point, the efforts of Karen Merritt Luebbert, Anne Moedritzer, and Elaine Harvey being especially valuable. The entire final manuscript was most proficiently typed by Ruth B. Southern of Brentwood, Missouri. Finally, I am most grateful to my wife, Jean, for her reflective and discriminating counsel in this undertaking, and for the forbearance she gently urged upon our children, Alice, Guy, Ann, Mary Anthony, Clare, Elizabeth, and now Suzanne.

**C. F.**

# CONTENTS

# The Grass-Roots Mind in America

# CHAPTER ONE

## INTRODUCTION: AN UNDERSTANDING OF THE GRASS-ROOTS MIND

### PRELIMINARY REMARKS

On the sultry evening of August 15, 1935, the nation languished in its sixth year of Depression. The dog days of summer had arrived, and as the temperature lingered in the nineties, people put fresh bowls of ice in front of their fans and relaxed beside the radio. They heard Lowell Thomas announce the news that President Franklin D. Roosevelt had just signed into law the historic Social Security Act. Later in the evening they heard Tommy Dorsey's trombone play the year's No. 1 hit, "Lullaby of Broadway," and still later listened to Kate Smith sing Hudson Motor Car sales to sharp recovery. Neighborhood movie houses featured the seven-year-old little girl sensation Shirley Temple, casting an image of adorable cuteness in *Curly Top,* and the twenty-four-year-old big girl sensation Jean Harlow, casting another kind of image in *China Seas*. In Detroit, heavyweight contender Joe Louis, the "Brown Bomber," was correctly predicting that Max Baer would be his twenty-first knockout victim in boxing's first major black-white confrontation in a quarter century. In Manhattan, at a Hotel New Yorker press conference, Senator Huey Long, "Kingfish" to his friends, promoted his candidacy for the 1936 presidential contest (he would be dead by an assassin's bullet in just twenty-six more days), while over at the Governor Clinton Hotel St. Louis Cardinal ace pitcher and talker Dizzy Dean groused about a fever that was "running over 110"—not high enough, it turned out, to prevent his shutting out the front-running Giants the next day to start their descent to a third-place finish. On the same evening four thousand miles to the northwest an Eskimo staggered up to the U.S. Signal Corps Station at lonely Point Barrow, Alaska, and gasped the words "Red bird smashed, bird men dead." A few hours later the duty sergeant keyed out the melancholy message that, indeed, William Penn Adair Rogers had perished in a plane crash into the shallow waters of the fifteen-mile-distant Walkpi area. And across the nation a people's spirits were a shade grayer.

Grass-roots America had good reason to mourn. Will Rogers was its legitimate spokesman, a man who reflected its mind as faithfully as anyone ever has. Moreover, he was wise, witty, and down-home-folks. When Rogers said there were some great people in the country, and they "ain't all on Wall Street, or at Luncheon Clubs, or in the Movies or in the Senate," [1] the men in the fields applauded. When he suggested that America forget about the League of Nations because "as long as we have seven million of our own out of work, that's our only problem," the men walking the nation's pavements heartily agreed. When he declared that "there is nothing as stupid as an educated man if you get him off the thing he was educated in," the folks in the towns breathed "Amen." When he spoke before a banquet of financiers and bankers and said "Loan sharks, and interest hounds: I have addressed every form of organized graft in the United States, excepting Congress, so it is naturally a pleasure for me to appear before the biggest," the men in the corner tavern nodded approvingly. And when he talked about the "American Animal"—the great majority—like this: "He don't seem to be simple enough minded to believe EVERYTHING is right and he don't appear Cuckoo enough to think that EVERYTHING is wrong. He don't seem to be a Prodigy, and he don't seem to be a Simp.

In fact, all I can find out about him is that he is just NORMAL"
—grass-roots America everywhere acclaimed his understanding.

So it was with the grass-roots mind, and so it is. It is a mind
of considerable steadfastness in the way it looks at the world;
it is a mind layered with trivia but bolstered by a hopeful resignation, a mind of staid judgment but easy credulity. It is an
unspectacular, unceremonious mind, and one that is peculiarly
unknown. It is a mind that moves not in the intellectual's fashion
of idea to idea but in the pedestrian mode of thing to thing, and
occasionally to idea. It is a mind that pulsates to a different
rhythm than that of its detractors: it "dances" rather than "races."
The metaphor is from G. K. Chesterton, who described those who
dance as moving around some central thing, "perpetually alter-
ing the attitudes, but perpetually preserving the balance"—the
movement is rhythmic and recurrent. Those who race "lose their
balance and only recover it by running towards some object, or
alleged object, manifesting precipitate or progressive movement,
because there is an unknown goal." The story to be told here
concerns those whose movement revolves around a pole of attraction rather than those who characteristically rush to things
on the periphery.

"Grass roots" is an American colloquialism that in dictionary
terminology describes something "close to, or emerging spon-
taneously from, a people." Allegorically—as it will be used in
the present pages—"grass roots" refers to people in the special
sense of those whose perimeters of life reach little beyond job,
recreation, family, media entertainment, and church, though not
necessarily in that order of importance. Their emotional life is
of far more importance to them than their intellectual life; most
often their attitudes reflect those of a major social group to which
they belong. Their occupations tend to be "blue collar," or, a bit
less often, "white collar," but the usual social categories of upper,
middle, and lower class are of limited usefulness in identification
of the grass-roots mind—value systems and mental orientation are
not closely proportioned to one's socio-economic level. Nor do the
terms "conservative," "moderate," or "liberal" mean much—because it is rarely doctrinaire, the grass-roots mind moves easily
from a very conservative position on one issue to a very liberal

position on another. All of this leads to a description that is essentially negative: the grass-roots mind is non-elite (by self-definition) and is on the lean side so far as formal education is concerned. It moves in a pattern of convention and stereotype rather than in a pattern of invention and careful distinction. Finally, it focuses on people, not on ideas.

Because it is the majority, the grass-roots mind is accorded a central place in the scheme of things—by politicians, by economists, by advertising agencies, and others. There are those who know it well, and in American society the people who know it best are usually those who have something to sell. A good merchandiser, having learned the hard way, can accurately assess the mass appeal of a new product. A discerning politician can *feel* a mounting ground swell long before a professional poll quantifies it. Managing editors have a great sense of the style level and the kind of content that will attract readers to the pages of their newspapers. However, the people who should know the grass-roots mind best—the educators—often do not. Their minds are necessarily preoccupied with "subject matter." Further, they have so many students in their classrooms that little time can be given to the peculiarities, the powers, and the failings of the strictly average individual. Whichever the case, teachers' insensitivity to the grass-roots mind is compounded by two much less appealing considerations.

Many teachers habitually carry in their heads a model of the human mind having "rationality" as its keynote, which is to say they see the usual course of its movement as orderly, progressive, and logical. This becomes a controlling assumption, mediating their professional enterprise and shaping their basic approach. The model has been greatly oversold. This book will question its validity, but for the moment it is enough to say that whoever accepts it is not very sensitive to, nor comfortable with, mental functioning that is far, far from the logical ideal, as is the grass-roots mind. Such inefficiencies as tangential thinking, stereotyping, whole-souled preoccupation with here-and-now realities, unreflective sentimental attachments, and fixed ideas of all kinds are distasteful to a committed rationalist and he often conveniently forgets their overwhelming dominance in ordinary society. His attitude is not quite as extreme as essayist Eric Hoffer says it is: ". . . scratch an intellectual [and] you find a would-be aristocrat who loathes the sight, the sound and the smell of common folk." [2] Nonetheless, there is a strain of truth to his view that intellectuals have a disdain for the lowbrow, practical mind.

In American education the rationalist understanding of human nature has been ascendant in the twentieth century, though sporadically it has been challenged by a romantic tradition. The latter has insisted that boxing the human mind into straight lines, squared corners, measured movement, logic, is to ignore much that is distinctively human—sentiment, imagination, creativity, eccentricity, passion, aberration. The student radicals of the 1960s saw things in this romantic tradition, objecting to the essential rationality of a system that operated by the numbers, by the rule, and by the book. It is ironic that they were most strongly opposed by a grass-roots America that itself prefers to operate within a romantic tradition, but a somewhat tighter one.

But if preoccupation with rationality deflects many teachers from an appreciation of the peculiarities and predictabilities of the grass-roots mind, many more are turned away by quite another factor, that of preoccupation with change. Around the turn of the century Henry Adams wrote that modern man had hold of a live wire that made him continually jump to its current but that he could not let go. The theme of the constantly jumping man is a major one in American life. On the everyday level it is manifested by a cultural preoccupation with "news," a word that in itself pretends change. On the political level it is reflected in the politician's response to every nuance of the sociological and economic indexes. On the philosophical level it delivers philosophers with no philosophy, only "logic." On the religious level it has begotten any number of priests and ministers eager to adjust doctrine to present public mood. On the social level it has turned out liberationists who see constitutional amendments as bringing a new Jerusalem. Finally, on the educational level it has produced a frame of mind that looks not to the constants of human nature but to presumed variables.

All of these basic attitudes derive from a preoccupation with change, a kind of eagerness for the new that weakens or even overwhelms a sense of the constant. The present, and the movement of the present into the future, comes to exercise a tyranny that warps perspective, often with the result that essences are lost sight of. One marches not to natural or historical rhythms but to the cacophony of what one sees as the present crisis. "Change" has become part of conventional wisdom, something of an "in" word that introduces thousands of lectures, articles, and learned analyses. There are several influences that incline a person decisively toward what may be called "change mentality." One of the most important of them is something that will be called here the "literature of change."

The literature of change is, as the term suggests, a literature that, in its enthusiasm or despair, abandons the past and intensifies the sense of the present or of the future, often with a "new world a-comin" sort of breathlessness. This change literature, so preoccupied with the swirl of NOW, too often ignores history, or what is worse, uses it.

The vocabulary of the historian has two overarching terms that comprehend the entire discipline: "continuity" and "change." Practically any primer of the craft deals extensively with these two notions. The prospective historian is cautioned to avoid the fundamental error of the "fallacy of presumptive change" as well as the "fallacy of presumptive continuity." [3] He is told that his task is to develop a habit of wider vision so that at the same time he observes and explains change, he gives appropriate emphasis to those forms that endure. In connection with the latter he is advised to keep in mind two principles that make human beings resistant to change: (1) that since it takes more energy to undertake the new ways than to retain the old, the latter have great staying power; and (2) that the familiar gives a sense of security that may make it preferable to a form that is admittedly superior in logic or theory. The total effect of these principles is summarized by historian Lewis B. Namier: ". . . the past is on top of us and with us all the time." The great practitioners of the historian's craft give this strong sense of pastness-in-the-present.

Unfortunately there are too few great practitioners, either within or without the discipline. The metaphor of the constantly jumping man has captured the perspective of writers from a wide variety of fields, with the result that everyone in the culture has been massively exposed to the literature of change. In time it has distracted educators from the unchanging. This literature of change is enormous, requiring careful attention to its many dimensions.

## THE LITERATURE OF CHANGE

It is seemingly characteristic of any age to regard itself as the ultimate in human experience. The past is but a benighted prologue to a present so different that it is as though dawn has come for the first time. Twenty-three hundred years ago the Greek historian Thucydides honored Athens as "the Hellas of Hellas" because in his day that city-state had brought to perfection all that was potential in Hellenic ideals. Several hundred years later at golden Rome the poet Claudian proclaimed that the gods had at last come home to rest in the city whose beauty and breadth were beyond that of "eye to measure or imagination to picture." A millennium passed and now the abbot Joachim of Floris announced that as of his day (late twelfth century) an age of sinful materialism had been superseded by the age of the Holy Ghost, bringing an enduring time when charity and love would reign supreme in human hearts. In the early years of the eighteenth century the French *philosophes* told Europe to have done with the Church—the great age of Reason had arrived, a time that "most nearly approaches perfection," and the human mind might now save civilization. About a century later the new day dawned elsewhere as Victorian England soberly contemplated its golden age of empire, reflecting on Shakespeare's hymn to English magnificence from *Richard II:*

This royal throne of kings, this scepter'd isle,
This earth of majesty, this seat of Mars,
This other Eden, demi-paradise . . .

Lacking deep historical roots, Americans have been particularly susceptible to visions of the glittering majesty of TODAY, with virtually every generation regarding itself as chosen by destiny. The exuberance of this nativist tendency is humorously, if ironically, recounted by historian Leland Baldwin:

A story is told about a party of Northerners who met in Paris at the close of the War between the States, to celebrate their victory with those sententious toasts characteristic of the day. Presently a Bostonian arose and in cultured accents offered the following:

"Here's to the United States, bounded on the north by British America, on the south by Mexico, on the east by the Atlantic Ocean, and on the west by the Pacific."

Next came a Chicagoan. "My eastern friend has too limited a view," said he. "We must look to our Manifest Destiny. Here's to the United States, bounded on the north by the North Pole, on the south by the South Pole, on the east by the rising, and on the west by the setting sun."

Prolonged and boisterous applause followed, but the next gentleman, a Californian, considered the toast too moderate. "With Manifest Destiny in our favor," he cried, "why limit ourselves so narrowly? I give you the United States bounded on the north by the Aurora Borealis, on the south by the Precession of the Equinoxes, on the east by Primeval Chaos, and on the west by the Day of Judgment!" [4]

These examples reflect a now mentality characteristic of the literature of change. In the cases cited the change has been of an extreme kind—from night into day, as it were, and in most cases the agent of change is not described. It is not to be supposed that most of the literature of change is quite so abrupt, nor is it inevitably a panegyric of present perfection. Many writers of the past century have seen it just the other way—that society has stepped into the quicksands of evil and will surely be corrupted or even vanish in short order. T. S. Eliot's *The Hollow Men* illustrates this genre, as does Oswald Spengler's *Decline of the West*. Cast in the same mold are some of the works of Henry Adams, H. L. Mencken, and Ezra Pound. But of this type, more later. For the present it is important to consider some of the underlying themes of modern literature of change.

For all those whose determination it is to demonstrate how unique is this twentieth century, especially in America, great multitudes of forces, causes, factors, and movements—agents of change—are available. They are strewn through social science and history books and classes, sometimes indiscriminately, as milestones in the march toward the present crisis or "Consciousness III." Most of them are facts—interesting, vital, and perhaps significant. The real question is what is to be made of them, beyond their influence on the distribution of power and wealth. For those of political bent the significant twentieth-century forces may include the decline of the boss system, the centralization of governmental authority, the rise of an activist Supreme Court, the extension of the franchise, and the image-making power of the media. Of importance to the economist are the concentration of business power, the development of countervailing force, the bureaucratization of American big business, the Keynesian revolution, and the components of economic growth. The sociologist depicts as influential such matters as the decline of the old status-holders, the alienation of the worker, the breakdown of the family, the depersonalization of culture, the institutionalization of prejudice, new mechanisms of role definition, and, along with the demographer, greatly increased mobility patterns of the American people. The historian of thought has a lengthy litany of isms that deserve attention: naturalism, neo-democratic idealism, pragmatism, racism, existentialism, subjectivism, conservatism, feminism, neo-orthodoxy, and there are others. No one can possibly run short of agents of change.

The change frame of mind entered into the American mainstream early. In the seventeenth century Puritans were fond of describing themselves as a society unmatched since the days of the first Christians. In the eighteenth century revolutionary patriots regarded their cause as Promethean: by 1776 Thomas Paine, in his electric appeal for separation from England, could use effectively the theme of America as a wholly new human experience where "an asylum" for human freedom might be established. American literature of the nineteenth century was dominated by the theme of the American as a "new Adam," somehow free from the tainted human nature of all who lived before him.[5] Nathaniel Hawthorne, Herman Melville, and Walt Whitman all savored this image of the American, their collected works a powerful argument for America having brought a new dawn. Of equivalent cultural importance were the nineteenth-century utopians, who foresaw an earthly paradise in America if only the right social or religious institutions could be devised. Dozens of models of the perfect society were invented and printed, many of them being given trials in such out-of-the-way locations as Oneida, New Harmony, Nauvoo, Red Bank, and Brook Farm. Indeed, so strong was the perfectionist movement that Ralph Waldo Emerson was heard to grumble that everyone in New England seemed to have a blueprint for a perfect society in his back pocket. Late in the century (1888) the popularity of Edward Bellamy's *Looking Backward* (which looked forward to the year 2000) further evidenced an assumption that human nature and the past might be repealed in America. After Bellamy, utopian projections went into eclipse, but surfaced again in the 1960s as a "now" generation went out to relearn the harsh lessons of reality in hundreds of experimental communes. The recurrence of such efforts suggests a continuing strength of the conception of the past as negligible prologue.

If utopian literature after Bellamy lost forcefulness, its weakening was more than made up for by a reciprocal rise of anti-utopian works, which themselves give great momentum to the change frame of mind. Anti-utopian novelists are just as apocalyptic as the utopians, but they see society going the other way, and fast, usually because of some structural ailment of the social or political body. Society's demise is not far off, or already here, in the framework of the story. Most students of anti-utopian literature trace its lineage back to the fantastic voyages of the late nineteenth century described by Jules Verne. But Verne's imaginative use of scientific contraptions only set the stage; the pivotal figure for development of anti-utopian literature was H. G. Wells.* Wells' first major work, *The Time Machine* (1895), was well-received critically, as were such subsequent works as *The Invisible Man* (1897) and *The War of the Worlds* (1898). Wells' influence was twofold: philosophically, he contributed to an attitude of "cosmic pessimism," according to which the evolutionary process was powerless to reverse the ingrained savagery

---

* Though most of the major anti-utopians have been British, their works sold well in the United States, and their influence has been very strong.

of human nature.[6] Thus, Wells advanced the twentieth-century assault upon the optimistic view that such contemporary forms as capitalism and democracy would inevitably bring a better world.

Wells' influence was also decisive in the creation of a new literary form: science fiction. Most of his work involved extravagant usage of mechanical and scientific principles, extrapolating them into the future to show the hideous fate toward which society is careening. On high literary levels Wells was followed by Aldous Huxley, who portrayed science-gone-berserk in *Brave New World* (1932), and by George Orwell, who in *Nineteen Eighty-Four* (1949) found totalitarianism to be mankind's most menacing enemy. On the popular level Wells' brooding contemplation of technological horror was translated into pulp fairy tales obsessed with gadgets and mechanical contrivances and, on the front covers, obsessed with semi-naked blondes. By the late thirties science fiction had branched out into the comic book field, into movies and radio. Whatever the aesthetic quality, the principle at bottom was the same: a major scientific or biologic innovation that restructured reality. Science fiction has been very popular in the United States, and by its general tone of overwhelming scientific advances has added substantially to an illusion of a changed world.

The literature of change crosses all academic boundaries. Its expression in fiction is rivaled in volume by what will be referred to here as sociological and environmentalist tracts, using both terms broadly. Apocalyptic in character and alarmist in tone, this literature is so vast that no man can read all of it in a year and a half.* Ordinarily it describes some disorder visiting the nation, which, if unchecked, will bring dissolution or even death. Society is sick, metaphorically at least. If anyone were to read regularly all of the major works, which, fortunately, few do, the effect would be to induce a kind of permanent siege mentality comparable to that suffered by overindulgence in watching popular

---

* I know because I tried. A long time ago, my doctoral dissertation involved categorizing such works. After a year and a half, my dissertation director told me to stop reading and start writing.

television newsmen. For this reason many who were otherwise put off by the naïveté of Charles Reich's *The Greening of America* (1970) found him oddly refreshing. In his variant of the "present crisis," the revolution had already occurred; now it was simply a matter of everyone, the older generation especially, coming around to accept "Consciousness III." Reich is, of course, an excellent exemplar of change literature: "From the perspective of history, change is coming with astonishing speed to the rest of the population as well." [7]

Though lacking any sense of history, doomsday sociology is often exceedingly colorful, which may account for its popularity. The superb prose of H. L. Mencken brought him millions of readers, even while he told them that twentieth-century American democracy had brought the reign of a mob whose intelligence was not above that of a goat. Van Wyck Brooks lamented that the "chill of the grave" had crept over American life, such that the individual, lacking access to a "collective spiritual life," was "either driven into the blind alley of his appetites or rides some hobby of his own invention until it falls to pieces from sheer craziness. Think of the cranks we have produced!" Sherwood Anderson eloquently described the spiritual emasculation and imminent physical impotence of the American male as the Machine Age overwhelmed him: "Can man, being man, actually stand, naked in his inefficiency before the efficient machine? Men, you know it cannot quite be done." Theodore Dreiser said that in his day Americans had come to be spiritual toads: "Strange, almost fabulous creatures have been developed here . . . men so singularly devoid of a rounded human nature that they have become freaks in the matter of money-getting." Following the success of his *Studs Lonigan* trilogy, James T. Farrell detailed the prostitution of capitalism and its final insult to the American people: the commercially inspired Hollywood confection, which once again told "the same old stupid and inept story of boy meets girl, framed, mounted, and glorified until it becomes a monumental absurdity." All of these writers are highly placed in the pantheon of American literary greats, and their rhetorical power has added significantly to a general preoccupation with change.

Recent evangelists of change are equally emotional, if less gifted in expression. They speak of "revolution" of one kind or another with wearying frequency. The old society is moribund, and a frightening tomorrow is nearly upon us. In the literature of change there are few moderate voices; it is a catalogue of hyperbole. Says John Platt, a physicist: "We are like men coming out of the dark house of the past into a world of dazzling sunlight. We have climbed up out of the dark cellar where we have been trapped for centuries, isolated, ignorant, selfish, combative, and helpless. Suddenly . . . we can see a vista of almost incredible knowledge, abundance, and well-being." [8] Writes American historian Ralph H. Gabriel: "The stirring and movement of no former age in our history can be compared with that of the middle decades of the twentieth century. Hurricane winds sweep across the American landscape. What the end will be only the future can disclose. But, as for the present, it is one of the supreme moments in history." [9] Even those whose message is essentially moderate inflate their rhetoric when the word "change" pops up. Witness political moralist John Gardner, who in *Self-Renewal* counsels renewed dedication to traditional values: "Decay is hardly the word for what is happening to us. We are witnessing changes so profound and far-reaching that the mind can hardly grasp all the implications." But even Gardner's prose pales alongside that of a group called "futurists."

The futurist cult, which has grown rapidly in recent years, has quickly acquired all of the trappings of scholarship, including a professional association, a bimonthly journal, and a book and film service. Its inroads into academia are manifested by any number of college courses across the land: Futurology 1, Futurology 2, etc.—they do not use Roman numerals. Quite recently Fairleigh Dickinson University in Madison, New Jersey, announced that it was institutionalizing the trend: a new academic branch known as the "Division of the Future" would open in short order. Journal articles of *The Futurist* have predictable (and predictive) titles: "Is Today Tomorrow?" "An Appetite for Evolution," "The Threat from Species O," "Tomorrow's Reform Agenda," and "An Answer to Monotonous Monogamy." Membership seems to be dominated by science-minded individuals who exhibit more than a hint of semi-religious millenarianism. Futurists have even enlisted some historians in their ranks, though the motivation of the latter seems unclear.

Futurists have certain evangels, who preach their gospel relentlessly. Kenneth Boulding is a major figure. An economist lately come to social dynamics, Boulding is the author of more than twenty books, some of them milestone works in the modern era. The opening lines of his 1964 production, *The Meaning of the Twentieth Century,* epitomize the extravagant *Weltanschauung* of the futurist: "The twentieth century marks the middle period of a great transition in the state of the human race. It may properly be called the second great transition in the history of mankind." Equally important in futurism is Alvin Toffler, a journalist whose *Future Shock* (1970) thrilled the faithful everywhere and made new converts to the cause. Though it was punctured by one reviewer as a "monstrous, mind-coshing, premeditatedly inexact, over-and-overstated and, above all, overlong tome," [10] the book was a success. It is an almost encyclopedic review of what Toffler regards as a sickness resulting from too much future too soon. It opens with the familiar verbal flourish—". . . the roaring current of change, a current so powerful today that it overturns institutions, shifts our values and shrivels our roots"—and closes the same way: "There is no facile way to treat this wild growth, this cancer in history. There is no magic medium, either, for curing the unprecedented disease it bears in its rushing wake—future shock."

Rivaling the eschatology of the sociologists are those who have come to be called the environmentalists. Here are ranged the plaintiffs against modern industrial society, finding cause against the state of the air, the water, the soil, thermonuclear energy, population, the oceans, and more. In his thoughtful book *The Doomsday Syndrome* (1972), John Maddox remarks that the men with sandwich boards proclaiming "The End of the World Is at Hand" have been replaced by a "throng of sober people, scientists, philosophers and politicians, proclaiming that there are more subtle calamities just around the corner." Further on, Maddox argues that these men of science are practicing "pseudo-science," reaching beyond their data to unwarranted conclusions, and expressing these conclusions in unscientific and flamboyant language. The present inquiry is not concerned with the accuracy of the scientists' claims, but Maddox is surely right in describing their language as extremist. A sampling: "portents of unprecedented disaster" (C. S. Wallia); "cancer of population growth" (Paul R. Ehrlich); ". . . prevalence of liver poison in the environment" (Rachel Carson); "The ecological facts of life are grim" (Barry Commoner); "the brink of ecological disaster" (the same).

Although not in the forefront of the hand-wringers, historians have contributed their share to a change-mindedness in educational literature. As a discipline, history has long been haunted by philosophic dispute over the historian's purpose. One school says his task requires him only to tell the best true story about the past. His calling does not require him to find some large scale pattern—whether progressive or cyclic—that makes explicable in a total frame all of the events and persons with which he deals. The other school wants the historian to say where a society has been and is going. At bottom the historian is to be a prophet, announcing to his readers the inner dynamic that drives society forward. In America, where the latter school has predominated, acceptance of its premise has meant that the historian either glorifies an increasingly "more perfect American democracy" or a more general "law of progress." Whichever the case, acceptance of the basic premise has brought the historian to a mental set that looks for change rather than continuity. Increasing the historian's tendency to be concerned with change has been an oddly acute jealousy of the brash "social sciences," which often tend to assume a predictive orientation. Such infidelity toward the discipline, said historian J. H. Hexter, "is sometimes accompanied by a shamefaced, somewhat exculpatory confession that history is a rather backward and low-grade science and by an expression of hope that when, if ever, it grows up, it will be able to predict future events." [11] Adding further momentum to the preoccupation with change has been the apostasy of the "New Left" historians, who no longer see their task as being to interpret the past, but rather to shape the future—to *foment* change, as it were.

The result of all this has been the production of a vast textbook literature of change at all levels. At the highest level the well-regarded economic historian Robert Heilbroner writes *The Future as History,* a compendium of historic change influences, which at its conclusion laments that too many Americans fail to appreciate the validity of the "law of progress." An equally respected historian, George Mowry, in his *The Urban Nation, 1920–1960,* finds that in the space of just forty years America had flip-flopped from an agrarian mentality to an urban mentality. At the middle level arrive college textbooks with predictable adjectives as part of their titles: "restless," "changing," "dynamic," "movement," "process," and the like. High school history books follow suit, though more slowly. Formal textbooks, having to please a conservative public, tend to a traditional though mildly skeptical Americanism, but most often "supplementary assigned readings" are decisively oriented to the change pattern. Generally reflecting this breeziness toward constants in the past is the influential National Council for the Social Studies (an NEA affiliate oriented to the secondary school), which, at its annual national convention in 1972, explored the general theme "We Live in a Revolution—Is Social Studies with It?" At lower levels the prevalent academic change-mindedness, filtered through a thousand student minds, eventually finds expression in a hundred-thousand articles, sermons, classrooms, and newsmagazines.[12]

Preoccupation with change is something of a general phenomena in the United States, being fed by a number of influences. Historical factors may be cited, including transcontinental settlement in a short 150-year period, the drawing in of millions of immigrants, and the rapid exploitation of rich American natural resources. Contemporary factors may be adduced, including the vast literature of change already discussed. Even psychological influences may be mentioned, such as the fact that "New!" is a proven commercial seller, and such as the fact that audiences, both classroom and public, are intrigued by novel ideas.

However understandable is change mentality as a general feature of American life, the fact remains that it involves a fundamental fallacy as regards the grass-roots mind. It assumes that the basic set of that mind has been or can be readily changed. But this is not true. The grass-roots mind changes at a glacial tempo, despite the swirling currents around it. It survives the rise and fall of idea systems, of doomsday forecasters, of charismatic personalities, of each new "alienated" generation, and of technological revolutions. It dwells in that fundamental inertia which, in the words of philosopher Morris Cohen, is as much "the first law of history as it is of physics." While intellectuals embrace the very latest in idea fashions and causes, the grass-roots mind remains anchored in its world of familiar people and familiar axioms. Indeed there is a good bit of cultural support for doing just that. It loves novelty, but wisely rejects it as a way of life. The story of the grass-roots mind is a tale of basic composure in the face of the wrenching influences of the twentieth century.

## ESSENTIAL FEATURES OF
## THE GRASS-ROOTS MENTALITY

In approaching the matter of the grass-roots mind, as good a place as any to begin is with the great novelist Joseph Conrad:

> . . . No, it is impossible; it is impossible to convey the life-sensation of any given epoch of one's existence—that which makes its truth, its meaning—its subtle and penetrating essence. It is impossible. We live, as we dream—alone. . . .[13]

The private world of a single human being is not really reachable by an explorer's pen. It has features of delicacy, of potential beauty, of fragility, of hidden vistas, of secluded corners, of solitary truth—these a great novelist might sketch, and then only faintly. It is altogether presumptive to try an unequivocal categorization and delineation of even a single human mind. What will be said here about structural patterns and tendencies of the grass-roots mind is meant to suggest not a stereotype but a setting, within which a potentially magnificent individuality may develop. Still, the charms of individuality, while they may obscure the basic tendencies, do not negate them.

The first thing to be said about the grass-roots mind is that it tends to operate within a narrow and highly personal frame of reference. Confronted by the demands of basic appetites, of work, and of surrounding social pieces—family, religion, television, organizations—it builds a peaceful, relatively enclosed world with just enough openings to allow the familiar things of life to come and go. The enclosure is not a cocoon, but more in the manner of a house, with openings of various sizes. The openings are of specific size and shape, cut to permit entrance by familiar people and things, and for novelties there is easy access into the vestibule. Rarely are the openings large enough to allow entrance of drafts of fresh air called scientific reasoning, but the grass-roots mind can get along without it because "horse sense" works well enough. If ideas wish entrance they had best come in concrete form and reveal their naked essence by very slowly paced degrees. By its owner's understanding, this enclosed world is thoroughly rational, and he knows that ideas will destroy a rational life. Thus, what is intended to close out external chaos also has the effect of closing out unduly novel ideas. Great forces of change may strike the external shell of this private world, but with surprisingly little effect. So bounded is its owner by persons and things and familiar ideas that either he cannot hear the roaring forces outside or he quizzically listens to them, makes of them a passing conversation piece, and then blandly dismisses them as not touching his own life very much. So too with the giant institutional abstractions—government and business bureaucracies —which, however much they tower over one's private world, are beyond his myopic vision.

All of the foregoing is an analogue, intended to manifest a basic insulated mode of looking at reality. But there are other aspects of the grass-roots mentality not communicable through this same analogy. The basic grass-roots views are a patchwork quilt of bits and pieces and oddments, which often do not match and may not have a unifying pattern. These views are gathered from every conceivable source, including, especially, popular proverbs, traditional folk culture, religious dogma, parental imperatives, small-town background, occupational values, mainstream Americanisms, military experience, popular culture hero models (about all of these, more later), but also including high school courses, newspaper feature articles, marital loyalties, and club interests, among other sources. In a curiously powerful way nostalgia enters in and contributes to the patchwork with wisps of imagery and barely remembered mottoes from the enchantment of youthful years. Basic grass-roots views may be regarded by a logician as a tissue of unexamined assumptions, half-truths, superstitions, and prejudices, some of them romanticized to the point of fantasy. Yet somehow they stand the test of reality and are accorded the status of infallible guides: Spare the rod and spoil the child, Hard work is the key to success, Nothing's too good for my kid, God helps those that help themselves, Experience is the best teacher, It's not what you know but who you know—and these "rules" are often validated in practice. These are but samples and obviously the content may vary. Some of these views are lightly held, perhaps only a tradition or a tentative grasping at a rule that serves well enough to keep out confusion; but most of them are strongly held, at minimum having a narcotic or occlusive effect and at maximum having the compelling force of revealed religion. The essential point of all this is the grass-roots tendency to elevate bits and pieces gathered from various sources to the level of absolutes, where they function as a web of controlling truths—the more so as one grows older. Finally, an obvious demurrer to the bits and pieces tendency occurs when an individual makes a whole-souled commitment to a dogma that has a broad, fully developed, and well-detailed philosophy of life. Mormonism is an excellent example of this, and so, in many cases, is the military life.

If the primary feature of the grass-roots mind is its propensity to construct a knowable and manageable psychic world, its second distinctive feature is its tendency to live in the present. It lives from moment-to-moment, from item-to-item, from person-to-person, from necessity-to-pleasure-to-necessity, from meal-to work-to shopping-to conversation-to meal, immersed in these as comfortable habits. In all of this there is little of thought except unbidden "pop-in" reflections, and little of analysis except according to established categories. There is negligible consciousness of the past as such, except a personal past, and little conception of or strong relatedness to the future, beyond hazy hopes and the anticipation of some personal pleasure shortly forthcoming. So pronounced is this foreclosure of the future that the grass-roots mind tends to take its pleasure now. This may mean impulsively "blowing it all" on a steak dinner, or a fancy outfit, or a new automobile, or on "something extra"—never mind that this necessitates future sacrifice. All of this reflects not so much a basic hedonism as an assumption that *now* is the important time, as recurrent appetites assert their demands; the life of the moment is too consuming to worry much about the future, which, one hopes, will go along something like the past. Meanwhile, since the grass-roots mind knows it is not ever going to make it big, why not chance a few dollars at the corner lottery shop and lightning just may strike. Very generally then, life goes on as an unplanned, short-term affair, daily, weekly, monthly, yearly.

The corollary of this is that life is a sensory, feeling, seeing, tasting, hearing, acting, and perhaps thinking thing. It is persons, bills, seasons, depressions, lively jokes, ball games, medicines, beers, and sex magazines, not ideas, theories, and conclusions. The grass-roots mind instinctively knows that life is far wider than thought, embracing far more than the mind can master. It is "too concrete, too rich, too unbounded" for logic to dominate. John Henry Newman put it this way: ". . . this universal living scene of things is after all as little a logical world as it is a poetical; and, as it cannot without violence be exalted into poetical perfection, neither can it be attenuated into a logical formula." What the grass-roots mind seeks is the direct and the concrete and something of a personalization of whatever is experienced. Television producers know this and thus fill their shows day and night with a texture of real life—the Archie Bunkers, the Waltons, and the soap operas all reflect it. Journalists know it, and use it to sell millions and millions of *National Enquirers, National Tattlers, People Weeklys*, and the like, each week. Admen know it and have been personalizing their products since the first Babe Ruth beer testimonial in the 1920s. Lawyers know that verdicts are reached on image as much as logic and organize their cases accordingly. Thoughtful students of politics know that grass-roots interests are personal, not political, and that therefore local issues and sometimes national ones are resolved by who lines up on which side, rather than by debate on abstract considerations. Grass-roots interest in Washington affairs runs at least as much to the private ones as to the public ones. Preoccupation with the concrete and the personal is a tendency reflected in daily conversation. What Richard Hoggart wrote about the English working classes is applicable everywhere:

The conversation . . . is almost always elemental, sometimes rough and often generous; its main themes are among the great themes of existence—marriage, children, relations with others, sex. . . . They are all doing what working-class people always do, wherever they find themselves and however unpromising their situation may appear; they are exercising their strong traditional urge to make life intensely human, to humanise it in spite of everything and so to make it, not simply bearable, but positively interesting.[14]

Summarized, the grass-roots mind leans on human connections, and on gossip—the latter written off by some as a negative feature of small-town life, but a characteristic of all grass-roots life, except that in the city it sometimes takes the form of reading gossipy newspapers and magazines.

It will not suffice, of course, merely to describe the grass-roots mind as dominated by concrete demands and interests and let it go at that, for there is another level of function of major importance. It relates to matters less temporal and less tangible, involving considerations of personal validity, basic values, private feelings, silent ideals, and, as many insist, conscience. At this level the grass-roots mind often manifests bone-deep insecurities, especially concerning ultimate questions. It gives the impression of being open on such matters, but is not really so; the impression of openness derives from the tendency to seek reassurance, which, given the grass-roots mind's consciousness of its limitations, it continually requires. In fact, at this level it is much less open than at the practical level described earlier. In its deeper recesses the grass-roots mind is quite intolerant of abstractions that explain without giving extensive emotional comfort at the same time. The intensely rational principles of the intellectual are suspect, and so is he, until he gives his principles a full grounding in human warmth and association. Put in another way, the grass-roots mind is very reluctant to substitute rational models for emotionally vibrant ones. Thus, at the deeper level, logic is a poor teacher; it asks for a surrender of too much that is grounded in flesh-and-blood experience. Here, then, at this level of the grass-roots mind is the seat of the sense of religion, which persists in common people long, long after their more intellectual contemporaries have dismissed the inspirations of these common folk as "passé."

Implicit in the preceding paragraphs but a distinct feature in itself is the grass-roots mind's devaluation of ideas or of the ideational life. It is not that ideas are necessarily disdained; rather it is that given the emphases already described, ideas rank low in the order of priorities of life. Life is too short to await "proofs" and too wide to entertain abstractions for very long. Native shrewdness reveals that action, not thought, is life's first imperative—to reason is not to *live*. Ideas are not usually necessary to occupational competence, which is the grass-roots mind's forte. Moreover, excessive theorizing may carry one away from his own nature, with its special necessities. Given this modest appraisal of the role of intellect, it is not surprising that the grass-roots mind has little interest in and scant facility for managing larger ideological patterns. It resisted school training in such matters and comfortably follows a concrete mode of thought, which does not augur well for an enlarged attention span. Its mental richness lies in its wealth of images; its effective functioning is heavily reliant upon them. The grass-roots mind is rarely comfortable with written expression that lacks pictorial power; effective sportswriters know this, as do novelists, and the editors of *Time* magazine in its earlier days. Generally, in word usage it prefers the policy of Will Rogers, who observed that "unfamiliar words were 'detour' signs to readers, who would cuss and take a different 'route' next time." The trouble with strange words, said Rogers, is that "You don't understand them, and they don't understand you, old words is like old friends, you know em the minute you see em."

The matter of "words" and their frustrations is of fundamental importance in understanding the grass-roots mind. The American literacy figure of 99 percent should be celebrated with certain reservations. The grass-roots American has a marked uneasiness in the presence of much written expression, expression, that is, that rides logic rather than people images, or that leans on conceptual structure rather than on familiar associations, or that simply lacks the texture of immediately recognizable life. Materials such as tax forms, employment application forms, even directions for preparing food, often present major comprehension problems.[15] Aware of such problems, newspaper editors modulate their papers' content and style accordingly. Still, it is worth noting that 50 percent of newspaper readers have trouble with the front page.

This discomfiture with certain kinds of written expression does not demean the basic intelligence of the grass-roots mind, though it may subdue it. As mentioned earlier, occupational competence is the home ball park of the grass-roots American, and within that ball park—be it dedicated to automobile mechanics, insurance adjustment, horse training, hardware store sales, carpentry, farm operation, secretarial work, stockroom management, truck driving, or the manifold tasks of the household—the visitor can expect to lose. Grass-roots intelligence thrives on its home grounds.

The ongoing mental life of the grass-roots American is much taken up with the demands of present work or the details of the current activity, as he(she) finds "horse sense" solutions to the problems of the moment. Or perhaps he engages in goodwill conversation, usually about the peculiarities of others, of the weather, of this and that. This is often no more than talk for the sake of talk, or for the sake of the warmth of human contact. But ongoing grass-roots mental life has, withal, an active private side that provides crucial daily sustenance: it woolgathers. It savors images of recent or anticipated pleasures; it forecasts appearances if some new item is purchased or made; it lingers over visions of success in love and in work; it identifies scapegoats for plans that didn't work out; it comforts itself with recollections of "pats on the back"; it drifts into reveries suggested by a few bars of music or wisps of news stories; it imagines the future of loved ones, especially children. Recurrently intrusive upon all of this meandering imagery are thoughts of familiar people and scenes of familiar places. Vagrant though these fancies may be, they are a major means of making one's personal world livable and secure.

What emerges from all this is not the "congenital imbecile" that H. L. Mencken so churlishly described, but rather a man who, having little attraction to ideas or to rational analysis, is often peculiarly confined to the mottoes and slogans—bits and pieces described earlier—even when these are not especially related to the question at hand. This is the reason why public-opinion polls, which purport to summarize the grass-roots mind, are of little value in really knowing it. When questioned, the grass-roots mind responds with an opinion, but since the opinion often has a vague foundation, the response is apt to be different next time, especially when the question is placed in a different context. Or, the response is likely to depend on the signals one has been receiving lately, and the grass-roots mind is especially vulnerable to reiterated expectations of what it should think on public issues, and to waves of popular sentiment.

Other vexations follow upon these characteristics. Being credulous, the grass-roots mind can be bamboozled not only by media and by politicians, but also by commercial promoters. Lacking intellectual flexibility, it is inclined to believe a clever saying repeatedly offered, as in advertising. In fact, massive and successful advertising campaigns have been mounted using just this principle, viz., "Everything's better with Blue Bonnet on it"; "It's Libby, Libby, Libby on the label, label, label"; and of course that Kentucky product that is "finger lickin' good." If the hard sell is done in the context of extravagant neighborliness—a real, down-home folksy approach—it becomes even more effective, so strong is the grass root's inclination to view favorably that which has a personal and friendly flavor. But there is one area in which the grass-roots mind cannot be fooled, that being art. No matter how insistently repeated, no matter how agreeably demonstrated, the idea that abstract art is really art is quickly rejected. Trusting as it does in the concrete and the sentimental, the grass-roots mind believes that art must first be representational, then perhaps mildly exploratory. It wants not what is new, but to be reminded of what is already known, and it helps if that familiar thing is sentimentally portrayed. Modern artists cannot accept this and are continually chagrined to learn that classic American landscapes are overwhelmingly the best sellers in discount stores across the land.

The peripheral role assigned to intellect by the grass-roots mind brings other correlates. For one thing, high intelligence takes on the garments of shrewdness in practical affairs or of great perceptiveness in dealing with people. Further, because of the narrowness of the conceptual base, the "food for thought" becomes not ideas but the problems, the patterns, the possibilities associated with hobbies, with odd jobs around the house, with sewing, with gardening, with outings, with domestic pets. Life is "privatized" in these ways. Much of leisure time is spent in "doing one's own thing." Finally, the nearness of personal horizons and the tendency toward the concrete bring a disposition to find heroes—kind of a yearning after some person who while being common clay has risen to the overarching achievement usually possible only in private dreams.

Here then is the grass-roots mentality: a mind that devises a private world for effective and meaningful interchange with on-going life, that lives and moves from thing to thing, that imbeds itself in layers of social thickness, that believes its perceptions in their concreteness provide a better key to reality than does abstract analysis, and that regards the world of the intellect as only one sector of a much larger spectrum that is total life. In short, the grass-roots mind uses its rationality selectively, applying it to goals that are emotionally chosen. It is a mind toward which young people gravitate as soon as they begin raising children; it is a mind in which an elderly America finds repose. If it is criticized for being infertile, as in ideas it is, then it is equally to be cited for its essential vitality.

This basic and winning vitality is reflected in the grass-roots mind's optimism that somehow things will work out. It is reflected in the ability to roll with the punches life delivers, adjusting expectations to fit concrete possibilities and personal limitations. It is reflected in the intuitive rejection of life-denying preachments by those who too far surrender to theorizing. Most of all it is reflected in an unpretentious self-respect, a quality most accessible to those who with courage have engaged life fully and sometimes failingly across a wide spectrum.

The grass-roots mind is every inch romantic, as such reflecting an American tradition that emerged as an articulate movement in the mid-nineteenth century. Romantics of that era, rebelling against the intense rationalism of earlier years, called for greater emphasis on passion and imagination and less on logic. They believed in innate wisdom; they found nature a more revealing source of truth than books; they stressed personal fancy and recommended full expression of the emotions. They counseled a fullness of concrete experience. They doted on imaginal flights, glorifying mystery, and folklore, and horror stories, and sentimentality. They decreed unremitting individualism and unrestrained freedom as the key to self-fulfillment. The grass-roots mind accepts all these prescriptions, modifying only the anarchic individualism to one that operates within the firm bounds of social convention. Thus, from the standpoint of the history of ideas, the grass-roots mind follows—though not consciously—a rich legacy of American thought.

The underlying theme of this book is the grass-roots mind's retention of a sense of absolutes in the face of all the changes and relativisms that vex the twentieth century, and which the literature of change so insistently says has brought a new dawn. In ways already described this sense of absolutes is grounded in certain fixed tendencies of the grass-roots mind. But change is unstintingly confronted in quite another way—by falling back upon specific ideas in which great confidence is placed. Just what these ideas are depends on what one hears in the media, where one comes from in the country, or what group one is loyal to in his daily life. It is to the first of these areas, that of the media, that this inquiry will now turn.

# CHAPTER TWO

## THE AMERICAN MIND AS SHAPED BY POPULAR CULTURE

**LEISURE AND THE RISE OF POPULAR CULTURE**

The great news story of 1914 was told in a series of headlines of increasing boldness across the front pages of *The New York Times:*

HEIR TO AUSTRIA'S THRONE IS SLAIN *(June 29)*

AUSTRIA READY TO INVADE SERVIA, SENDS ULTIMATUM *(July 24)*

AUSTRIA BREAKS WITH SERVIA; RUSSIA IS MOBILIZING HER ARMY *(July 26)*

KAISER CALLS ON RUSSIA TO HALT WITHIN 24 HOURS *(July 31)*

GERMANY DECLARES WAR ON RUSSIA *(August 2)*

The dreaded confrontation had begun, and for four years the world's newspapers would talk of little else. Perhaps no event of the modern era can rival in historic significance the incidence of World War I. Yet, another event of 1914 was of the same classic importance, though it received little attention at the time. It reached the front page on January 6, then vanished into the business and financial pages, rarely to reach major news status again. *The New York Times* account of this event follows:

### GIVES $10,000,000 TO 26,000 EMPLOYEES

Detroit, Mich., Jan 5. Henry Ford, head of the Ford Motor Company, announced today one of the most remarkable business moves of his remarkable career. In brief it is:

To give to the employees of the company $10,000,000 of the profits of the 1914 business, the payments to be made semi-monthly and added to the paychecks.

To run the factory continually . . . by employing three shifts of eight hours each. . . .

To establish a minimum wage scale of $5 per day. Even the boy who sweeps up the floors will get that much.

The news hit the business community like a bombshell. Predictions of Mr. Henry Ford's bankruptcy were freely made; others expressed dark presentiments over the future of capitalism. An Indiana newspaper reflected the views of many when it commented that of course workers should get higher wages, and "it ought to be warmer in the winter and cooler in the summer, too."

But Ford's vision surpassed that of his critics. The eight-hour, five-dollar day that he inaugurated made of American capitalism a different breed than it had been before. Not only were labor-management relations raised to a new *détente,* but most of all the old-fashioned capitalism of fierce selfishness was destroyed by Ford's move. Now workers, the "oppressed" in Marx's lexicon, would have "a piece of the action," and would, moreover, because of increased income, become excellent customers of their "capitalist masters." Indeed, it is not too much to say that by his bold stroke Henry Ford "broke the mainspring" of traditional capitalism and completely foiled any Marxist hopes of a revolutionary America.[1] Ford's announcement was of the first order of importance, but not only because of its economic implications. By leading the way to the eight-hour workday, with a resultant increase in workers' leisure time, he made them much larger consumers of culture.

As adoption of the eight-hour day gradually widened in ensuing years, idealists were hopeful: with increased leisure time now might come the glorious day of the withering away of ignorance. Museums and galleries would be filled, libraries and schools crowded, with seekers after the best that the world's thinkers and artists had thought and said and painted and portrayed. But it did not happen that way. Instead, the ball parks were filled, along with the theaters, movie houses, and taverns too. Book and magazine circulation increased enormously, but of these far more were about Tarzan than about philosophy. Sales of pictures greatly increased as well, but they ornamented the front covers of pulp magazines. Americans had become voracious culture consumers, but it was culture of the popular kind.

The increased immersion of the average American in "popular culture" is important because of the conditioning effects it has had upon the grass-roots mentality. In the preceding chapter a brief outline was given of the political, economic, social, and intellectual forces that have influenced this century. These forces have been important, but the *really* important fact of the American twentieth century is how little affected by these forces has been the grass-roots mind. It was as though this mind was insulated from impinging shocks of reality. Popular culture has played no small part in supplying the insulation materials.

Everyone has his good reasons for seeking escape. They extend across the entire band of human experience, and the list is as lengthy as that of personal goals unsuccessfully sought, or of disappointments borne, or of illusions shattered, or of unpleasantness endured. "Human kind cannot bear much reality" said T. S. Eliot, cannot and will not. When the tolerance level for reality is reached, relief is no farther away than the television switch, or *True Romances*, or *Jaws,* or many parts of the daily newspaper, a cornucopia of popular culture. Such things provide an anodyne and an opportunity to wander through a predictable and satisfying landscape. Trash? Often. Trivia? Frequently. Relief? Always.

The question of how popular culture is best described has haunted the literature of the subject for the past twenty years. Early commentators tended to dismiss it as rubbish, claiming that it reduced its presentation of experience to the lowest common denominator and thus vulgarized the aesthetic and emotional sensibilities of its audience. Bernard Rosenberg is representative: after pillorying "sleazy fiction, trashy films, and bathetic soap operas, in all their maddening forms," he concluded, "mass culture threatens not merely to cretinize our taste, but to brutalize our senses while paving the way to totalitarianism." [2] Other observers often reacted more gently, pointing with hope to the many oases in the supposed wasteland of popular entertainment. It was not until the mid-sixties that the defense caught up with the offense, so to speak, and popular culture was given generous praise. Predictably, it was couched in the neoromantic terms characteristic of the time. Speaking of the development of a "new sensibility" rooted in modern technological society, Susan Sontag redefined art as an instrument for "modifying consciousness and organizing new modes of sensibility." [3] In this framework, popular culture—some of it—was seen as valuable for its potential of stretching the senses, e.g., atonality in music, unpatterned color combinations in art, formlessness in modern films. More recently, some scholar-observers of popular culture have insisted that aesthetic evaluation of any particular media product, such as *All in the Family* or *Deep Throat,* is philosophically unsound. They argue that aesthetic reaction is entirely and legitimately an individual matter, being founded on the extent to which any given experience elicits a compatible "fantasy" in one's mind. In this view a critic may analyze favorable or unfavorable public reaction to a production, but not judge the production itself to be "good" or "bad" by any objective standards.[4]

Whatever the justification of popular culture the fact remains that most of it is not at all memorable, not at all original, in sum, not at all art. There are several reasons for this, most of them residing in the nature of the relation between the audience and the producer. On the one hand the audience comes to the production—television show, magazine story, motion picture, whatever—often fatigued by routine or by frustration. It is suffering, one might say, from a surfeit of the here-and-now and craves relief, not inspiration. On the producer side there are several factors at work that bring about standardization of content. Unlike the traditional artist whose audience glorified individuality of vision, the creator of today's fare faces an audience seeking escape. His future depends on how well he provides it. He knows that escape fare is not simply the building of dream worlds; much more often it is the presentation of a theme of life that is very familiar to the audience, stories of love surviving difficulties, of the return of a prodigal, of virtue triumphant. In presenting such stories he satisfyingly confirms the experience or at least the ideals of his audience.

Even if a producer were to have ambitions to great creativity, there are important factors that operate against him. The media is a hungry master whose appetite runs far beyond the delivery capacity of any creative artist. Further, technical and cost considerations often severely limit artistic range. Finally, much of what is called popular culture is commercially sponsored, and few companies can afford the risk of offerings that challenge traditional verities and values.

As a result of all these influences, popular culture is formula-ridden. The same plots, the same characters, and the same messages are heard again and again. In the view of essayist John Cawelti, all cultural products may be seen as a compound of invention and convention, the latter being things known beforehand to creator and audience, as plots, character types, and themes. Inventions are new conceptions by the creator. In popular culture conventional components dominate heavily, of course, representing "familiar shared images and meanings" and promoting cultural stability.[5] The concept of formula (as just described) is important in twentieth-century America, Cawelti points out, because, with the weakening of religious unity, the formula products of the media have become increasingly the bearers of cultural values, the carriers of the wisdom of the people.

Generally, then, popular culture has played a major conservative role in American life in the twentieth century. It has supplied the insulating material against unsettling currents of reality. If in the daily news vice is triumphant, in popular culture virtue conquers; if villainy achieves mastery of public affairs, courage and honesty endure in the popular fray; if depravity characterizes many private lives, morality and righteousness significantly inform life in popular culture. If, as some contemporary observers insist, modern life has brought chaos, that chaos is closed out in popular culture, where the old axioms still prevail. These observers pay too much attention to forces that swirl outside the house. If they were to look inside they would find that the mental furniture of the grass-roots mentality remains quite antique. The themes and views of life whereby this furniture is continually renewed through popular culture will now be explored.

## DOMINANT THEMES

"Popular culture" is a term of very wide applicability. As used in these pages it includes the offerings of television, radio, motion pictures, the theater, magazine fiction, best-selling adult literature, popular records, comic strips, and children's and adolescent literature. It also includes popular social organizations, spectator sports, and quite importantly, popular philosophy. An examination of the output from these many sources evidences three dominant themes or idea clusters: emphasis upon individualism; legitimacy of traditional American values; optimism as a basic assumption of life. The discussion that follows will concentrate upon each of these themes in turn, but it is not to be inferred that each has a separate existence from the others. In many productions the three are interwoven; in others strong emphasis upon one theme precludes direct attention to the others. Thus what will be described here is not consistently a one-piece pattern, nor is it a universal pattern. But it is a recurrent pattern, supplying ample material for development or elaboration of a fixed system of ideas.

### Individualism

The ideal of individualism is deeply rooted in American economic, political, and social life. It flows as a core theme through American literature, language, history books, theories of character, slogans, and, predictably enough, popular culture. Of its several meanings the one appropriate to the present discussion relates to the capacity of the individual to shape his own destiny, to control his fate by drawing upon inner resources. In this light individualism becomes a matter of a personal battle against forces, both good and evil, which continually seek full domination over one's life. Because contemporary life has brought organization systems that imply such domination, presentation of the principle of individualism in popular culture has often meant a return to the American past. There was a time when an open and virginal country drew forth those with the initiative and courage to master it. And so, presentation of the theme of individualism has involved an American pastoral.

The pastoral is a narrative return to a simpler life, most particularly to a life close to nature. It glorifies that earlier time as a golden age when virtues were more sharply defined, emotions more honest, personal relations more concrete, and conflict more unequivocal than is possible in the present complexity. The pastoral is a literary convention through which an artist presents his views on human perfection and imperfection. Most often the pastoral work uses a rural setting, but this need not be the case. What is central is that the artist present oppositions, either expressed or implied: on one hand is complex, usually urban, society, with its sophistication and artificiality; on the other hand is simpler, usually rural, society, with its freshness and its earthy quality.[6] The basic emotion animating the author's view of the simpler society is nostalgia.

In America the pastoral has not required much stretching of the imagination. It was not very long ago that the simpler life prevailed throughout the land, and as recently as yesterday in many places it prevailed still. It does not require much dreaming for millions of individuals to project back to a day when an individual might take his fate in his hands, and through his own resources do with it what he would.

By far the widest usage of the pastoral is the western in its several forms. In popular fiction the twentieth-century exemplar was Zane Grey, who wrote upwards of sixty books with a total sale (as of 1972) of more than twenty million copies.[7] The West as drawn by Grey was a hard and lonely world, but one which conferred a certain nobility upon those who could meet its challenges. The virtues that counted in the contest were the simpler ones—physical hardiness, courage, determination—and what did not count at all was intellectuality, or spirituality either for that matter. Woman's mission was the basic one of bearing and raising children who as adults would stand fast when challenged by adversity. In general, Grey presented the West as a purification setting where only those with individualist virtues were capable of withstanding the trial.

Hundreds of other western novelists have repeated Grey's glorification of individualism, matching him in returning the reader to a simple, clear-cut, and very demanding world.

The rise of the motion picture industry in the 1920s brought further exploration and development of the pastoral motif. In thousands of western movies and serials the struggle was desperate, but the end the same: through his resourcefulness and skill the hero gained the victory, or at least held off the forces of evil until the law arrived. The impression of the hero's self-sufficiency was often deepened as he rode off into the sunset—alone. During the fifties and sixties variants on the western theme appeared, with the hero sometimes being shown to have certain undesirable traits, such as Bart Maverick's gambling habit. Still, when he got into full stride against the forces of evil, there was no doubting his personal effectiveness.

It is not to be supposed, however, that media producers have limited themselves to the western in representing the American pastoral. The attractions of the small town were thoroughly explored by film makers of the thirties and forties. Almost invariably the town milieu emerges as the source of the hero's strength and as the implicit victor when the hero defeats the massed forces of the city. The bitter commentary upon the narrowness and hypocrisy of the small town initiated by Edgar Lee Masters in *Spoon River Anthology*, and by Sherwood Anderson in *Winesville, Ohio,* did not often reach the screen. Idealization of village America was not quite so pronounced in the sixties and seventies, but the pastoral theme has remained alive. Even such non-status quo films as *Midnight Cowboy, Alice's Restaurant, Easy Rider,* and *Medium Cool* may be seen as reiterations of the excellence of simplicity.[8] Animating these productions are assumptions that insight and wisdom spring from association with nature, that natural man is superior, and that the city is an evil sink of corruption.*

The pastoral setting as fertile for the development of individualist virtues has been so heavily used in American popular culture that it has come to stand for those virtues. Presentation of the sim-

---

* There is, of course, an opposing media image of rural America, in which the small town is depicted as a hotbed of corruption and vice. See p. 63.

pler life, whether it be in the form of western prairies or television hometown type shows, serves to strengthen and reinforce listener awareness of individualistic qualities that have traditionally dominated in such settings. Furthermore, it is not only the action-serving virtues of individualism—agility and ingenuity—that are involved. The loose organization of western and small-town life provide maximum "social space" for the indulging of what might be called "the peculiar virtues"—eccentricity and a kind of innocent orneriness as manifested by character types on the old *Gunsmoke* show. In all, the pastoral creates (and re-creates) in America a world where individualism is the key attribute.

Individualism as a social ideal finds strong support in other facets of popular culture. It resonates throughout what cultural historians have called "self-help" literature. Back in 1899 a young (43) minister named Elbert Hubbard wrote a short story called "A Message to Garcia." This story did not initiate the self-help genre—Benjamin Franklin had seen to that—but it vastly widened it. Upwards of thirty million reprints of Hubbard's tale were distributed throughout the land, and young men everywhere vibrated to the theme that "Civilization is one long, anxious search" for individuals possessing initiative, courage, and resourcefulness. The stream of self-help literature expanded enormously in the twentieth century, studded with the writings of Andrew Carnegie, Bruce Barton, Russell Conwell, and, later, such authors as Norman Vincent Peale and Napoleon Hill. Each of these men had a somewhat different formula for success, but the principle was inevitably the same: personal and financial triumph depend on calling forth the rich resources that lie within each individual. The works of all these writers were highly popular with grass-roots America, each of them having sales well into the millions.

Looking at the sports side of popular culture it is evident that the principle of individual initiative has been and continues to be of decisive importance. It is true that insistence upon "teamwork" echoes through a thousand locker rooms and is re-echoed in ten thousand sports reports. The athlete is publicly measured by his willingness to sacrifice in the interests of the team, and the bleachers reverberate with boos when he places himself above it. Yet the individualist virtues still somehow put teamwork in the shade. In professional football the resourcefulness and daring of the Roger Staubachs, Fran Tarkentons, and Terry Bradshaws, in seeming individual combat against eleven fierce enemies, make nonentities of the linemen that protect them. The savagery of a defensive tackle's charge through three blockers is much more stirring than a triple-team block that puts him down. In a way appreciated only by aficionados of the sport, the great coaches of the modern era—Vince Lombardi, Don Shula, Frank Leahy, Woody Hayes, and others—have never sought to make "teamwork" their exclusive goal. Rather, they have sought to prepare individual initiative so that it might be exercised at the most useful place and moment of contact. What emerges from their coaching is the disciplined "tough guy" who can impose his will upon events. Simply because he *does* impose his will on events, the "tough guy" competitor—tough by way of strength, ingenuity, endurance, or courage—captures the imagination and loyalty of the grass-roots multitude. In baseball he is a combative Bob Gibson or Luis Tiant, in hockey a hard-nosed Bobby Clarke, in golf a modestly talented but determined Gary Player. The list of admired "tough guys" can be extended well beyond sport: in politics, Harry Truman; in battle, General George Patton; in movie westerns, John Wayne; in civil rights, Martin Luther King, Jr.; in affliction, George Wallace; in consumer protection, Ralph Nader; in international diplomacy, Patrick Moynihan. Very generally, such individuals reflect an assertiveness against odds that is held in high esteem at the grass-roots level. A famous coach put it this way: when the going gets touch, the tough get going.

Cultural endorsement of individualism is broad and deep, running well beyond the exemplifications given it here. It comes in through the pores and cracks of the entire social structure—in short conversations, in personal advice, in front-page stories. It is sufficient to say that no young American can grow up without massive exposure to individualism as a social ideal.

### Traditional Values

In the early 1920s British writer D. H. Lawrence, novelist, expatriate, and iconoclast, published a study of great American literary figures. It is not an unforgettable classic, as some of his other works are described, but it is memorable in one respect: it contains one of the few attacks in print upon the image and the influence of the great American philosopher-statesman Benjamin Franklin. Franklin is an authentic hero—not the father of his country, like Washington, nor its savior, like Lincoln, but certainly its sage and universal teacher. It is no small matter to tilt with him. But D. H. Lawrence did, and, although his attack was brushed off by Americans, he must be given credit for his exact aim.

Lawrence bitterly criticized Franklin because that venerable old squire had "set up the first dummy American." What Lawrence was speaking of is the influence that Franklin's ideas have had upon the American character. In 1759 Franklin published *Poor Richard's Almanac,* a popularly phrased guidebook for achievement of fortune, goodness, and fame. Poor Richard advised his readers to go to bed early and get up early, and they would become "healthy, wealthy, and wise"; he suggested that they "Waste not, want not"; he pointed out that "the used key is always bright"; and he preached that "God helps them that help themselves." Lawrence rightly recognized that these little homilies, and dozens more from the Franklin pen, are immensely important in American culture. Lawrence further lamented that he too had been poisoned by Franklin: "And probably I haven't got over those Poor Richard tags yet. I rankle still with them. They are thorns in young flesh." [9] But he is on guard now, "Oh Benjamin! Oh Binjum! You do NOT suck me in any longer." Unfortunately, Lawrence continued, the same cannot be said about the American people. They are corralled by these insidious little rules and motivated by them: ". . . America lies on her muck-heaps of gold, strangled in her own barbed wire of shalt-not ideals and shalt-not moralisms. While she goes out to work like millions of squirrels in millions of cages."

When the story of the little man in America is told from its beginnings, the name of Benjamin Franklin will dominate its pages. What Franklin did through his lively aphorisms was to establish rules for living for the American people. Working with the famous thirteen Puritan virtues,* he created a popular philosophy that rivaled the Bible in its impact upon the mind of the grass-roots American. With his allusions to nature ("The sleeping fox catches no poultry"—what clear talk to a nineteenth-century American), his easily remembered rhymes ("for he that goes a-borrowing goes a-sorrowing"), and his pragmatic values ("Plough deep while sluggards sleep, and you shall have corn to sell and to keep"), the Franklin gospel spread throughout an uneducated America that needed rules to live by. The simple and consistent structure of the Franklin "system" held a great appeal to all classes of Americans, schooled and unschooled. The Franklin rules became the guiding lights of the rather closed system of ideas that governed a rural people. They became the commandments of one's youth, which were carried in his head, and used, and then implanted into the minds of his own children. Franklin is so deeply imbedded in the language that his words will live as long as it is used in America.

If there were some young Americans who did not learn from parents that "Diligence is the mother of good luck" and other Franklin counsel, they certainly could not have missed getting the moral message from other sources. In the last half of the nineteenth century close to one hundred million McGuffey readers were printed and passed from hand to hand in American grade schools, each one of them containing moral advice similar to the Franklin epigrams. If somehow Johnny still didn't get the point, there was still another powerful voice. Between 1867 and 1899 Horatio Alger, Jr., wrote some 106 juvenile books, each of them proclaiming the same tidings: that the keys to success are industry, thrift, and determination, along with a modicum of luck. Circulation of Alger's books was simply prodigious, with one of his biographers estimating that as many as fifty million Americans had read at least one of his books.[10] The literary quality of Alger's prose was dismal, and by the early 1900s teachers and librarians were dismissing his works from their shelves. But paperback editions costing a dime brought booming circulation until the time of the first world war.

* The list: Temperance, silence, order, resolution, frugality, industry, sincerity, justice, moderation, cleanliness, tranquillity, chastity, humility.

Horatio Alger died in 1899, but his spirit lived on. In the mid-1880s a twenty-five-year-old New Jersey shopkeeper named Edward Stratemeyer submitted a story for boys to a Philadelphia publishing house. It was accepted and became the first production of a fabulous writing career. Young Stratemeyer soon went to New York, where he obtained a writing position with Street and Smith, the largest publisher of pulp magazines in the field. Within a few years Stratemeyer reached a milestone of personal achievement: he was asked to ghostwrite several new titles in the Alger series, which was much too profitable to discontinue after the originator's death. Eventually, Stratemeyer contributed eleven books to the series, writing comfortably in the same ethical vein as his predecessor.

But Stratemeyer's major success was still before him. Using his own name he had published in 1899 *Under Dewey at Manila Bay*, an adventure story about two young lads on a battleship. It sold very well, and he followed it with another topical book, *A Young Volunteer in Cuba*. This too was a hit, and now the "Old Glory Series" was well under way. And so began the niagara of Stratemeyer-produced books that were to spread-eagle the juvenile publishing field for nearly a half century. Using sixty-five different pseudonyms the "Stratemeyer Book Machine" turned out more than eight-hundred books for juveniles between 1899 and 1930,[11] when Stratemeyer died a wealthy man. The list of his series titles is seemingly endless, but some idea of his range can be gained by mentioning a few of them: The Rover Boys, The Motor Boys, The Bobbsey Twins, The Nan Sherwood Series, The Bunny Brown Books, The Dave Dashaway Series, The Tom Swift Series, The Hardy Boys, and of course, Stratemeyer's second all-time best seller, The Nancy Drew Series. The latter alone has sold more than thirty million copies, being surpassed only by the Bobbsey Twins. Together his five most popular series have sold about 125 million copies. So popular did the Stratemeyer books become that an extensive 1926 survey of schoolchildren found 98 percent of them favoring some one of his books.[12]

The importance of all this lies in the ethical models thus tendered to American youth. Any reader of a Stratemeyer book, any of them, can testify to the sterling qualities of the hero. He was truthful, honest, and courageous, obedient, fair-minded, and loyal. If a girl, she was bright, truthful, and graceful, pretty, popular, and perceptive. These are not exactly the same virtues as those preached by Benjamin Franklin, of course, but they are close. However, the really central impression left by the Stratemeyer hero is more important than any particular virtue cluster. That central impression is one of righteousness, and all of the traditional virtues are implicit in that notion. Arthur Prager, Stratemeyer's major biographer, provides a sample of this righteousness in an excerpt from *The Rover Boys on the Farm*. Dick, Tom, and Sam Rover are near the scene as a bully menaces a young lady:

> As they looked into the [candy store] they saw Tad Sobber reach over the counter and catch the girl clerk by her curls. He held fast, grinning into her face, while she tried to pull away from him.
>
> "The mean wretch!" cried Dick. "He tries to make himself as obnoxious as he can to everybody he meets."
>
> "Oh please let go!" came in the girl's voice through the open doorway. "You hurt me!"
>
> "Don't worry, I won't hurt you," replied Sobber, still grinning.
>
> "But I-I don't want my curls pulled," pleaded the frightened girl. "Oh please let go, won't you?"
>
> "I want you—" began the bully, but did not finish, for at that moment he felt Dick's hand on his ear. Then he received a yank that pained him exceedingly.
>
> "Ouch!" he yelled, and dropped his hold of the girl. "Oh my ear! Dick Rover what did you do that for?"
>
> "I did it to make you behave yourself," answered Dick sternly.[13]

Edward Stratemeyer was preeminent in the field of juvenile literature, but he was not alone in it. Other authors whose books regularly appeared were Ralph Henry Barbour, Gilbert Patten (using the pseudonym "Burt L. Standish" he wrote the Frank Merriwell Series), Lester Chadwick, Matthew Colton, and Clair Bee. All of these writers used the sports story as their medium. An analysis of the sportsman's code enlightening such stories was done by Walter Evans in the *Journal of Popular Culture*. Evans prefaces his account with a comment from George Orwell, indicating the great importance of juvenile stories:

> Personally I believe that most people are influenced far more than they would care to admit by novels, serial stories, films, and so forth, and that from this point of view the worst books are often the most important, because they are usually the ones that are read earliest in life. . . . Here is the stuff that is read somewhere between the ages of twelve and eighteen by a very large proportion, perhaps an actual majority . . . including many who will never read anything else except newspapers; and along with it they are absorbing a set of beliefs which would be regarded as hopelessly out of date in the Central Office of the Conservative Party.[14]

In his analysis of the works of sports fiction Evans found that the sportsman's code is something of an unwritten set of rules and behavioral expectations among those youths who "live for the game." Given this devotion, the young athlete is pure, a dictum extending to avoidance of alcohol, gambling, smoking, and nearly all girls (the exceptions being *the* girl and mother); he is modest to the point of self-effacement; he is self-reliant but also self-sacrificing in the interests of the team and the school. Generally, the code by which the sportsman lives is "invariably stricter than the ethical standards of society in general." Evans' survey of the literature of boys' sports fiction covered a period of more than one hundred years, and led him to this conclusion: "It is fascinating that in spite of distinct variations in plot, character, and setting through the years the unwritten sportsman's code has remained almost unchanged. The basic tenets and function of the code in *Tom Brown's School Days* (1857) are virtually identical in *Throw the Long Bomb* (1967)." [15]

The recommended virtues of juvenile literature have been reinforced by membership in any of the several large youth organizations to which young Americans may belong. The Boy Scouts of America began as a national movement in 1910, received a federal charter in 1916, and grew rapidly in popularity in ensuing years. By the mid-thirties the organization had yearly membership of more than a million boys, with an accumulated total membership since 1910 of nearly seven million.[16] By the mid-fifties yearly membership exceeded two million, with more than twenty million past members. As of 1973 yearly membership exceeded five and a half million, and more than forty million young men had been registered scouts. It is estimated that the *Handbook for Boys,* the official publication of the Boy Scouts, has had a total readership of more than fifty million boys, and, as of the mid-1950s, was reportedly second only to the Bible in all-time American sales.[17]

Scouting ideals are described by one historian as "these odd, old-fashioned things." The scout promises to keep himself "physically strong, mentally awake, and morally straight." Personal qualities to be sought include trustworthiness, honesty, thriftiness, and reverence. To advance to a high level a boy must demonstrate increasing achievement of these ideals, as well as skill and handicraft accomplishments. In the past sixty years Boy Scout organizations have demonstrated over and over that their allegiance to their ideals is not mere lip service, as their members have received many honors for unselfish community service. That scouting ideals have character-shaping influence is affirmed by historian Will Oursler as he recounts this incident:

> In a town in Texas some years ago, a young boy set out on "The First-Class Hike"—a fourteen-mile hike that was the last test a Second-Class Scout passed before he advanced to the rank of First-Class Scout. The day was hot, blistering, and dry. The boy had been out a couple of hours. It was nearly lunchtime.
>
> When the boy's father came in for the noon meal, the mother reminded him that their son was out hiking over the dusty Texas roads in this terrible heat. "I've fixed a Thermos of lemonade," she told him. "Why don't you drive out there and take it to him? He's somewhere on that road. I'll bet he's thirsty."
>
> The father agreed. He put the lemonade in the car and drove off in search of the boy. Ten minutes later, the car was pulling up alongside of a very bedraggled, sweaty, dirty-faced boy.
>
> "Look what I brought you, son," the man said. "I'll bet you can use it."
>
> He brought out the lemonade. The boy's lips broke into a grin and then the grin faded. "Look, Dad," he said, drawing back. "I

can't have any of that. I'm on my honor to take this hike without anyone helping me. Even giving me a drink of water."

For an instant the father looked surprised. Then his hand with the lemonade drew back. He looked at the dirty face of his own son. "Sorry," he said. "Sorry. I didn't understand. But look—Mom fixed this for you. So we won't tell her about it, will we? We'll get rid of it and it'll be our secret."

The boy nodded and they understood each other, and the man said, "It must be a pretty wonderful organization that teaches a boy to have moral fiber like that."

And a young army officer whose name was Dwight D. Eisenhower drove off and left his boy John to finish his hike entirely on his own.[18]

It is not possible to measure the impact of the Boy Scouts upon American culture. But given the leadership potential of its members, the intensity of their commitment to ideals, and the large number of men with a background of scouting, there is more than a little basis for saying that the Boy Scouts "helped to shape the destiny of one hundred and fifty million Americans." [19]

The most popular girls' organizations, the Girl Scouts of the U.S.A. and the Camp Fire Girls, promote ideals very similar to those of the Boy Scouts. The Girl Scout Law requires a member to be honest, fair, to help where she is needed, to be cheerful, friendly and considerate, a sister to every Girl Scout, to respect authority, to use resources wisely, to protect and improve the world around her, and to show respect for herself and others through her words and actions. The Camp Fire Girls' law is less extensive as to the virtues to be cultivated, but requires that a member "Seek beauty, give service, pursue knowledge, be trustworthy, hold on to health, glorify work, be happy." In explanation of this law the national organization emphasizes spiritual development as essential to its members. Thus, "Each part of this Law is related to ethical living. . . ." Membership in the Girl Scouts by 1972 had risen to more than three million; Camp Fire Girls' enrollment in the same year was approximately 750,000. Along with the Boy Scouts, these organizations continue to provide further cultural underpinning for classic American virtues.

The education of American youth to the traditional virtues has been a massive enterprise, extending through parental discipline, school training, juvenile fiction, and youth organizations. As adolescents matured into adulthood they found the same themes repeated throughout the culture, reinforcing what they had learned earlier. Of particular importance in this connection were three cultural agents: the early twentieth-century Chautauqua institutes; the vast body of adult fiction; and the ascendant electronic media.

The Chautauqua institute flourished from its beginning in 1903 until the great expansion of the radio and film industries in the late 1920s. It was a sort of traveling community college to rural America. Named for its place of origin in western New York, the Chautauqua operated on a circus principle, complete with tents and brass bands, bringing teachers, entertainers, public-issue speakers, and literary figures to small towns of from one thousand to twenty thousand people. The "show" would continue for several days, and then move on to the next town on its circuit. Small-town America loved it: in 1924 Chautauqua institutes attracted thirty million Americans (one-third of the population) in twelve thousand communities to their proceedings. Reflecting its Sunday church-school origins, the Chautauqua glorified traditional American values, specifically those of domestic fidelity, public morality, clean living, and genuine neighborliness. There was also an abundance of patriotic fervor woven into the lengthy daily programs. All of this was just too much for eastern intellectuals, whose movement away from the American mainstream was well under way by the late 1920s. Said one of them sourly, "Naturally the Chautauqua idea grew up in the forests and on the prairies, not in the cities. . . ." [20] But for the most part their hooting went unnoticed in the round applause given Chautauquan ideals.

As grass-roots Americans found more time on their hands in the twentieth century, they read more newspapers, especially of the tabloid variety, and much more fiction, especially as found in family type magazines. Such magazines as *The Saturday Evening Post, Colliers, Women's Home Companion, Ladies' Home Journal, McCall's,* and *Good Housekeeping* through the twenties and thirties achieved circulation advances well into the millions. All of them featured bland short fiction with clearly defined heroes (more often heroines) whose virtue was beyond question. The principle of selection for *The Saturday Evening Post,* for example, was the extent to which an author assumed the validity of accepted moral values and built his story from there. A survey of values characteristic of mass-circulation magazines during the 1921–40 period found that heroes and heroines "became vehicles of long established values." [21] Apparently this tendency has continued in the remaining family magazines: a survey of *Good Housekeeping* magazine fiction from 1965 through 1969 found that the moral system taught by the stories was decidedly conventional.[22]

Nor did readers of the "more or less" sex magazines of an earlier day get other than a fairly straitlaced view of life. The covers of such magazines as *True Story* beckoned browsers with promises of sexual excitement, as suggested by fetching poses and hints of illicit liaisons—"The arms that held me were not my husband's," etc. Yet inside the covers the "confession" story strongly promoted conventional morality. In a survey of the late 1960s researcher David Sonenschein analyzed seventy-three fictional pieces from eight romance and confession magazines. The predominant subject matter of the stories related to sex, as one might expect. But if the thirteen and a half million readers of these magazines were looking for libertine morality they were disappointed. What they got was domesticated sex. According to the researcher the thematic direction of each of the stories was toward stabilizing one's personal life, searching for a way of living in which sex harmonizes with the basic demands of psychological health. Sonenschein found it very obvious that the stories were founded on traditional axioms: marriage, family, love. These are presented as the stable blocks upon which a satisfying life may be built. Thus, the point of view of the confession magazines is decisively conservative. The survey concluded with this summary:

> Contrary to our initial expectations, then, the romance magazines really appear to be paragons of virtue, arguing with a traditional cultural morality for the necessity of love and the family and the

minimizing of sex if one is to survive personally or socially. The effects and consequences of acting outside these values are spelled out in a fashion that explicitly details the risk. For the reader, the result is not a pretty picture.[23]

Best-selling novels, at least until the 1950s, similarly espoused traditional virtue. Best-seller lists of the thirties and forties were crowded with stories that found religious and domestic morality as the key to a satisfying life. Pearl Buck's *The Good Earth* dramatized the values of industry, frugality, and familial tranquillity, making it to the top of the best-seller list in both 1931 and 1932. In 1935 Lloyd Douglas became the most popular novelist in the country with his *Green Light;* his popularity was buttressed by the earlier *Magnificent Obsession* (1929) and later best sellers of 1943, *The Robe,* and 1948, *The Big Fisherman.* All of Douglas' works emphasized altruism and the Christian virtues, and by 1965 had combined sales of more than nine million. Other top best sellers in the same vein were James Hilton's *Good-bye, Mr. Chips* (1934), A. J. Cronin's *The Keys of the Kingdom* (1941), Franz Werfel's *The Song of Bernadette* (1942), Russell Janney's *The Miracle of the Bells* (1947), and of course the millions of Zane Grey and Max Brand westerns and the millions upon millions of Erle Stanley Gardner mysteries.[24]

The radio and motion picture industries achieved great cultural importance during the late twenties. Both mediums assumed a stance strongly supportive of status quo morality. This was especially evident in daytime radio, which soon became heavily dominated by coast-to-coast soap operas. By 1940 there were eighty-one dramatic serials in daytime hours, drawing the rapt attention of forty million listeners. These "domestic novels" of the air specialized in crisis—familial, financial, romantic, medical—with every Friday bringing a super-crisis to carry listener interest through the weekend. The standard format for the fifteen-minute soap opera provided for several bars of theme music, a minute of advertising, thirty seconds of explanatory prologue, eleven minutes of drama awash in emotion, a minute more of ads, thirty seconds of tease for tomorrow's episode, and again the theme music. The dramatic situations generally took place in the home of the heroine, with resolution of the problems of exotic disease, vanished husbands, corrupt in-laws, or financial distress, proceeding inch by talkative inch. Sometimes it took an entire eleven-minute segment for the decision to be made to call a doctor about a strange pain in the back. As the heroine survived the daily crises she manifested again and again trustworthiness, ingenuity, and steadfast religious faith, regularly dispensing cracker-barrel truths to those suffering through the crisis of the moment. Scriptwriters faithfully reflected their public's moral leanings, and if they sometimes grew restive, there was one agency that had a rule requiring some "God-stuff" on every third page of the script.

By the early twenties there had emerged from Greenwich Village and from college campuses something called the "new morality," which expressly denied the validity of traditional virtues relating to sex. For a time Hollywood dabbled in the new morality, but it was not long before public pressures brought a retreat to conventional standards. In 1922 the industry established a production code that carefully circumscribed what might be shown on the screen. The code, plus the fact that films were less an art form than a business—making the producer especially responsive to pressure from organized social groups—resulted in a Hollywood product filled with stereotypes manifesting traditional values. The Hollywood "good girl," however dubious her principles might appear in the early reels, turned out to be a wholesome, generous, love-and-marriage type who with her winning ways domesticated her somewhat wayward boyfriend. The Hollywood hero was epitomized by Clark Gable, whose native American appeal went with "popcorn, horseshoe games, and BVD's"—and

> . . . that face—ears, eyes, dimples, and all—is the face of the good-looking fellow in the next block. It is essentially a small-town face, although its owner has learned to slick back his hair and wear evening clothes. It bears the unmistakable look of the native good fellow—a Mason, an Elk, who might stand for a popular athletic coach, or be chosen as Scout Master to take the children on a camping trip. Although now groomed and made familiar with night-clubs, as the movies require, this is the same fellow who used to bring his girl a box of candy every Saturday night.[25]

Inevitably, the hero walked in the pathway of virtue, though this feature was sometimes obscured by the characteristic emphasis upon his individualistic attributes. He was a man whose courage and eventual decisiveness won the victory over any foe. Later on came variations in the pattern, as with the tough-guy roles of Humphrey Bogart and James Cagney, those model free agents who specialized in knocking the opposition flat. In the final reel, though, they invariably showed their integrity to principle. Still later came heroes of the James Stewart, Gregory Peck, Henry Fonda variety. They were still larger than life, but reflected a certain diffidence of manner, along with an awareness that not all of life's problems could be solved "by a breezy manner, a gun, or a punch in the nose." [26] Physical force had given way to psychological force, but underneath it all the same classic virtues furnished the motivating power. Nor did the film ethic change much in the post-World War II era. A study of American films from 1946 through 1969 found them to be essentially conservative: "Most films of the period, both successful and unsuccessful, distinguished and undistinguished, reinforced, extolled, illustrated, reflected, and transmitted dominant cultural orientations. . . ." [27]

Other media forms have also carried the traditional message, if often less decisively. On the Broadway stage a mid-century vogue of American folk tales set to music, such as *Oklahoma! Bloomer Girl, Up in Central Park,* and later, *The Music Man,* fulsomely glorified an earlier day and its singular virtues. Studies of the comic-strip ethic, as manifested in Tarzan, The Phantom, Mary Worth, Gasoline Alley, Rex Morgan, M.D., and even Superman, have repeatedly shown an exaltation of simple virtues.[28] The vast playground of television has reflected a decided tendency to confirm conventional values in its viewers, and the greater the involvement with it, the greater the conventionality.[29]

Much contemporary cultural comment has it that American entertainment industries have abandoned the emphasis upon traditional values in favor of frankly libertine morality. But a closer look suggests that while sexual promiscuity is more openly explored in the media, traditional values remain dominant, even if the rationale for them has shifted from a religious to a psychological base.

Especially is this evident in the modern soap opera. Soap opera is nothing more than popular fiction, and as such relies on what one observer describes as conventional ideology, which is to say "a body of assumptions and attitudes which commands immediate, emotional and inarticulate assent, as opposed to a set of ideas which requires self-conscious and deliberate intellectual formulation. Fiction, in general, depends upon a community of such belief. . . ." [30] The reader (or viewer) of popular fiction is told a tale that gives concrete expression to the accepted ideology, with right-wrong tags being made unmistakably clear. Since many in the modern world are preoccupied with psychological health, modern soap opera puts its right-wrong tags in a psychological context. Thus, virtue is not to be sought because of its implications for salvation (the preoccupation of an earlier generation); it is to be sought because continued sexual infidelities will bring intolerable psychological loneliness in their wake. Transient intimacies may be excused, but, in the long run, only enduring unions hold promise. Virtue remains the best policy, but with the moral equation expressing a different product than before: "Loving + mating = happiness to avoid loneliness." [31]

Much other popular fiction reflects a similar pattern. On magazine racks alongside such shabby pornography as *Penthouse* and *Hustler* are dozens of the highly popular "gothic novels"—suspenseful stories, usually about women, characteristically set in secluded and frightening old mansions. Almost invariably an attractive and tradition-minded heroine is pitted in a love contest against a beautiful but sexually wicked villainess. Sexuality itself is not put into question; in fact, its attractions are frequently highlighted, but in proper subordination to other values. What *is* made clear are the unhappy consequences when the woman—the wicked one—loses control over her sexuality. She becomes unhappy, often vicious, and occasionally even a murderess. In summary, the gothic novel upholds as ideals such "traditional values as marriage and motherhood as ultimate goals for women, the superiority of domesticity over sexuality, and the feminine responsibility for nurturing and maintaining the family unit." [32] Farther on down the magazine rack is the display of "love comics," which are aimed at the early teen-age girl. Here the road to happiness is similarly posted. The young reader finds the "plain girl" heroine to be a model traditionalist, rejecting drugs, women's liberation, and premarital sexual adventures in favor of marriage and family. Love comic stories, said one student of them, give explicit endorsement to the cluster of virtues often associated with an earlier "small town" America.[33]

Those who make much of striking contemporary instances of immorality, of unusual sexual liaisons, or of fancied new ethical modes, and predicate a new order based on such observations are too often ignorant of the working of the ways of our ancestors in and through the culture. These forebears speak with powerful voices of the validity of classic virtue—through standard language aphorisms, through established hero models, through song, through standard plot forms, through folk tales, through generally what may be called "oldies but goodies" of every kind. What a people thought and believed in a nation's past has far more compelling power, in the long run, than any preachment of a "new gospel" for today.

### Optimism

Beyond its external appearance, underneath its manners, its morals, and its values, any culture gives off a rhythmic beat that comes closest to revealing its soul. In America that beat, that vibration translated into terms of a fundamental assumption, is that life is a happy thing, a promising thing, a thing wherein God is in His heaven and with Americans, too. Its corollary is that evil has no permanent place in life, only entering into it as an occasional interloper. Some years ago, in *The American Adam,* R. W. B. Lewis interpreted nineteenth-century American literature as reflecting the basic American view that here in this country was brought to birth a new Adam, the essential American, untainted by the past and by past human folly. He was innocent, and in the richness of his innocence, he viewed life trustingly and with a good deal of buoyance. He regarded proclivity to evil not as a basic ingredient of human nature, but only as a temporary condition that could be readily crushed by decisive action. Lewis' symbolization of the American-as-new-Adam is one of the great informing insights of American cultural history. It helps explain, for example, the American's devotion to the principle of individual-as-agent for destroying evil. It helps explain the American inclination to view America as virtuous vis-à-vis other nations. It clarifies the basis for the American's almost complete lack of a tragic sense:

> Our Perry Masons, our Napoleon Solos, our Matt Dillons, all live in a world that is violent without being tragic. They dare much, but they risk little, because they operate in a blandly optimistic world where every catastrophe has a happy outcome. As savior-images they are shallow and immature conceptions, reflecting a broad-based lack of realistic vision in the society that breeds and cultivates them. If our popular heroes are going to achieve stature and dimension . . . they will have to shed their shining invulnerability and step cautiously into the broad horizon of tragic experience.[34]

American optimism reverberates throughout the culture. It is the professed philosophy of community organizations, some of which even go by the name of "Optimist Club." It is an unspoken assumption underlying the huge amount of installment buying that fuels the American economy. It is the password to success according to "self-help" advocates. It is the key weapon in the ad writer's arsenal of sales-promoting ideas. It is a constant voice in American folk wisdom and folklore. It is the point of view that dominates American history textbooks and animates a major school of American historiography.[35] It is the presupposition of American liberalism, the basic underpinning of American glorification of education as a panacea, and the distilled theme of American religion over the past century. Its philosophical expression—perfectionism—is the fundamental moral commitment of the American people.[36] Given optimism's negative component—the absence of a tragic sense—it helps explain the American tendency to purchase elaborate funerals and the propensity to shunt the aged and the dying to a secular limbo. American optimism is not, of course, the same as the British Boy Scout law which requires that "A Scout Smiles and Whistles under all circumstances." * Yet this seeming immoderation of British Boy Scout law does have a counterpart in American culture. It is not so far back to Snow White's seven dwarf friends who sang the highly popular "Whistle While You Work," which was followed, in 1945, by Johnny Mercer's "Accentuate the Positive, Eliminate the Negative." The perceptive musical comedy team of Rodgers and Hammerstein seemingly noted the cultural attractiveness of such songs: for *South Pacific* they wrote "A Cockeyed Optimist," for *Carousel,* "You'll Never Walk Alone," and for *The King and I,* "I Whistle a Happy Tune."

An optimistic point of view is something Americans understand, and want, and need, and will pay for. Awareness of this truth has built many fortunes in the twentieth century, none of them larger, perhaps, than that of William Roy DeWitt Wallace. In 1920 young Wallace got the idea of selecting, condensing, and reprinting colorful articles from the thousands of American periodicals. Editors of most of these publications were delighted to get the free publicity that the reprints would bring. Putting about thirty of these reprints between heavy paper he called his brainchild *The Reader's Digest.* Sales went well, rising to nearly three hundred thousand by the end of the decade, to more than two million in 1939. By 1956 circulation had reached ten million, and by 1973 *The Reader's Digest* was purchased monthly by more than eighteen million Americans. It is an amazing success story, an achievement well deserving the jealousy that dominated the attitudes of competing magazine editors. Yet Wallace's formula was not fancy. It included simplism (in style), dogmatism, and most of all optimism. The editors saturated the magazine with success stories, accounts of human compassion, revolutionary medicines, new inventions improving the quality of life, light anecdotes, sketches of charismatic personalities, and accounts of

---

* The law is elaborated as follows: "Scouts never grouse at hardships, nor whine at each other, nor swear when put out, but go on whistling and smiling. When you just miss a train or someone treads on your favorite corn—not that a Scout should have such things as corns—or under any annoying circumstances, you should force yourself to smile at once and then whistle a tune, and you will be all right."

community cooperation. Observing that the *Digest* seemed to have something good to say about nearly every facet of life, including racial problems, sickness, old age, and death, one critic disgustedly complained that optimism "drips from every issue as sweetly as syrup from a maple tree." [37] To some the *Digest* may have been saccharine and stultifying; but to many, many others it provided monthly confirmation of roseate expectations.

For much of its life Hollywood has specialized in sentimental romances, in happy endings, generally in presenting a cheerful view of life. Nowhere was this tendency more fully developed than in the work of Walt Disney. His major cartoon characters—Mickey Mouse, Pluto, Goofy, Donald Duck, and others—radiated warmth and good humor, some occasional mischief notwithstanding. Villains are overdrawn, possessed of monstrous evil, with few or no redeeming features. So distinct is this pattern that clearly, in the Disney view, evil is outside the cultural mainstream, rather than in the typical human heart. Disney productions have a scrubbed look, a moralistic flavor, and, inevitably, a happily-ever-after ending—on the order of Mary Poppins (1965), which may be regarded as a prototype. One critic lumps Disney with such other smiling faces as Dwight Eisenhower, Hubert Humphrey, Norman Vincent Peale, and Pollyanna.

But Walt Disney is more than simply a purveyor of happy children's stories, folklore, and animal tales. He symbolizes a major facet of the American character. Disney catered effectively to the American predisposition to treat reality somewhat more favorably than it deserves to be treated. Illustrative of the rose-colored view characterizing Disney works was the remodeling of the Grimm Brothers' fairy tale *Snow White*. In the original Grimm story blood flowed freely, with a climax of torturing the wicked queen by forcing her to dance to her death in red-hot iron slippers. But an expurgated version issued from the Disney studio: the scenes of violence and the moments of sadness were sharply reduced and the execution of the witch eliminated; the seven anonymous little fellows in the original were given charming names—Doc, Happy, Grumpy, Sneezy, Bashful, Sleepy, Dopey—and far more important and very humorous roles, so much so that "And the Seven Dwarfs" was added to the original title; the ending saw Snow White and her prince singing a joyful song as they faded into the distance.

The bowdlerizing of the classic paid dividends. Within six months of its release *Snow White and the Seven Dwarfs* repaid studio costs of its three-year production phase. Its first-run gross amounted to well over $8 million, and by the mid-1960s it had delivered more than $22 million to the Disney account. Disney had struck a master chord on the American keyboard. This chord continued to resonate with further productions. The enormity of the Disney appeal is suggested in the following statistics (world figures, but with heavy American totals):

> In 1966 Walt Disney Productions estimated that around the world 240,000,000 people saw a Disney movie, 100,000,000 watched a Disney television show every week, 800,000,000 read a Disney book or magazine . . . 150,000,000 read a Disney comic strip . . . and 6.7 million made the journey to that particular Mecca in Anaheim, insistently known as "Walt Disney's Magic Kingdom" in the company's press releases and more commonly referred to as Disneyland.[38]

The phenomenon of Disneyland (and now its Florida equivalent, Disney World) is well worth exploration in the context of the American habit of optimism. Disneyland is purer "Disney" than any of his film productions: during his later years he continually tinkered with it to make it reflect more exactly the smiling view of life that was his trademark. Among the most important features of Disneyland in the present connection are the following: an image of happiness, as manifested by the endlessly smiling employee faces, their hospitable ways of speaking, and by the cartoon characters who meander among the crowds; an image of extreme cleanliness, carefully maintained by nightly hosings (gum is even scraped up), by nightly repainting of gun targets, and by costumed maintenance men who collect tons of trash and garbage each day—all of these practices soften the squalid and homely aspects of life; an image of an earlier, happier America, as suggested by the five-eighth scale size early twentieth-century main street, by use of fifteen-foot embankments walling off the outside world with its mass of poles and wires, and by the various "lands"—Fantasyland, Frontierland, etc., which promote a nostalgic return to real and imagined scenes of youth. Disneyland is an exact mock-up of its creator's view of the inner world of the grass-roots American. That this view has accuracy is shown by the numerous millions who visit Anaheim each year, as many as half of them returnees.

As might be expected, intellectuals, nearly all of them, fulminate against Disney, his works, and all his lands. Adjectives like banal, packaged, tawdry, dangerous, immature, dehumanizing, nightmarish, and the like resound through the critical literature. But the withering attacks of Disney's enemies cannot hide a fundamental truth perhaps best expressed by a recent critic as he laments, "The Disney label inspires certainty, trust, and belief in many Americans confronting a chaotic, 'immoral,' survival. To such believers, a Disney 'revival' brings the same surge of hope and sense of insurance as was brought by the great evangelists of the nineteenth century." [39]

The optimistic cast of mind in Americans has other manifestations. It fosters a diffuse romanticism that works its way into major experiences as well as the cracks and corners of day-to-day living. By "diffuse romanticism" is meant a tendency that at once places emotional experience at the apex of existence, venerates the sentimental, and comforts itself with nostalgia. Of such a tendency is the American romantic love complex born. Americans, many of them, "fall in love with love," giving it a dreamlike quality wherein the attractions of the beloved are so glorious that negative possibilities are completely ignored. Among the component elements of the romantic love complex are the beliefs that happiness is inevitable in true love regardless of problems, that to be truly in love is to be in love forever, that for each person there is only one true love for a lifetime, that love is an all-or-nothing feeling with no in-betweens, and that when one is in love the beloved becomes his (her) only goal in life. This is not the place to argue the truth or falsity of these propositions. Of present importance is the observation made by an anthropologist that such glorification of love as a key institution is an extremely rare cultural phenomenon, having existed only in modern urban

United States, northwest Europe, Polynesia, and the European nobility of the eleventh and twelfth centuries. Moreover, said the same anthropologist, it is a frame of mind that correlates positively with a clearly conservative value structure.[40]

In America the romantic love complex comes to life in many radio, television, and motion picture products. But its clearest voice is found in the popular ballads of the thirties, forties, and fifties. Semanticist S. I. Hayakawa explored this theme some years ago, reporting that according to his analysis of popular songs the love-struck American lived in a strange and trying world. For one thing there was "an enormous amount of unrealistic idealization . . .

Will I ever find the girl in my mind,
The one who is my ideal?" *

This perfect woman has never existed, but when she is approximated

"I took one look at you,
That's all I meant to do,
And then my heart stood still . . ." †

The love that follows has a euphoric setting, and no economic problems disturb the bliss:

"We'll have a blue room, a new room, for two room
Where every day's a holiday, because you're married to me." ‡

Unfortunately the course of love does not run smooth, and after a spat, self-pity sets in:

"I'm all alone every evening
All alone, feeling blue,

* "My Ideal," by Leo Robin, Richard Whiting, and Newell Chase, Copyright, 1930, by Famous Music Co.
† "My Heart Stood Still," by Lorenz Hart and Richard Rodgers, Copyright, 1927, by Harms, Inc.
‡ "Blue Room," by Lorenz Hart and Richard Rodgers. Copyright, 1926, by Harms, Inc.

Wondering how you are, and where you are,
And if you are, all alone, too." §

Awash in distress, the lover withdraws

"I'll never love again
I'm so in love with you
I'll never thrill again
To somebody new . . ." ||

And retreats to the nursery:

"I'm going to buy myself a paper doll to call my own
A doll that other fellows cannot steal. . . ." #

All of the lyrics above are Hayakawa's illustration of "love's unhappy progress." [41] But they could be multiplied at will by a diligent researcher. In an overall way what is important in Hayakawa's illustration is the further light it throws on the American tendency to close out the unpleasant realities of life in favor of the happy view. Much contemporary popular music, notably rock, blues, and country and western, with its contrived electronic sounds and fulsome private emotion, similarly condenses life to a sort of euphoric float trip.

Romanticization of conventional experience is nothing more than a grass root's fondness for imaginal flights combined with an extension of basic optimism. The "gilding" of reality occurs naturally enough. If one accepts the premise, even implicitly, that evil is not integral to life, there is no reason not to have large expectations of it, at least until one is bloodied by adversity. Optimism brings a vaguely favorable mental disposition, which sets the tone of all experience that follows. And the same optimistic cast of mind, oriented to the roseate, brings also a decided tendency to relish and persevere in substitute worlds that everyone in some way builds in order to make the external world livable.

§ "All Alone," by Irving Berlin. Copyright, 1924, by Irving Berlin.
|| "I'll Never Smile Again," with words and music by Ruth Lowe. Copyright, 1939, by Pickwick Music Corp.
# "Paper Doll," by Johnny Black. Copyright, 1915, by E. B. Marks.

Popular culture catches people in their most relaxed moments, when they are defenseless, so to speak. It shapes them, or perhaps more exactly, confirms them in the shape that other facets of culture have already created. The pattern described in these pages—individualism, traditional virtue, optimism—is integral to the grass-roots mind, continuing to inform it, and in a way uplift it. Whoever would know that mind must begin with popular culture; but he must not stop there, as there are other influences of strong forming power.

# CHAPTER THREE

## GEOGRAPHICAL MENTALITIES

### THE SMALL-TOWN MIND

#### Extension of the Small Town
#### into Modern America

The volume of effort expended by Americans in scrutinizing the distresses of urban living is enormous. Almost without fail any given issue of a national newsmagazine abundantly describes some new urban stress that threatens to become a crisis. Radio and television are necessarily not as verbose, but no less on the verge of panic as the casualties in the streets mount. More cerebral but equally passionate are the college professors, who hinge intricate solutions of urban emergencies to "new sociological perspectives." Any librarian can tell of stack rearrangements made necessary by the increase in urban literature.

All of the concern may be necessary and proper, but its preponderance serves to obscure a basic fact: that America is not an urban nation, not entirely, perhaps not even mostly, from the standpoint of psychological orientation. The most recent statistics —the 1970 census—put 26.5 percent of the population in rural areas. In itself, one-fourth of the population is a hefty percentage, but the truth of the matter is that the percentage is much higher. The Census Bureau defines rural areas as those of less than 2,500 population that lie outside metropolitan areas. Thus left out of the rural count are literally hundreds of towns and cities beyond the urban fringe whose psychology and point of view are decisively rural. To be precise, thus excluded—unreasonably and in some cases reasonably—are 1,874 communities with population in the 2,500–5,000 range; 1,115 communities in the 5,000–10,000 range; 646 communities in the 10,000–25,000 range; and 205 communities of 25,000 or more. In these 3,840 communities are found more than thirty million people, or 15.2 percent of the total population.[1]

But one might lose the argument over definitions and thus be forced to grant that the 2,517 citified folks of Tarkio, Missouri, along with the 31,269 sophisticated souls of Grand Island, Nebraska, should be counted in the urban population of the United States. In this case the percentage moves back toward the one-fourth figure. However, the rural world remains undiminished. Twenty years ago historian Richard Hofstadter wrote that America was born in the country and has moved to the city, going on to say that it has never forgotten its country origins. Hofstadter said this of late nineteenth-century America, but it still has much truth. Millions of today's suburbanites came from the country and settle down as close to it as they possibly can, as do many of those who grew up in the city. Further, according to a recent Department of Agriculture survey, some forty million of city and suburban folk would "prefer to live in a rural or small-town environment."[2] It is not only the tangible violence of the city that motivates this preference; it is also the deadly image of the city portrayed in American films of the past twenty-five years.[3] Then, after the movie is over, the city dweller goes home and reads a local newspaper account of the famous psychiatrist Dr. Karl Menninger describing the city as "a very unhealthy place": ". . . most psychiatrists would say that, however commendable the social impulses that have some influence in creating the cities, maybe the city dwellers overdo it a little bit and that, as far as mental health is concerned, farmers have it all over city people." [4] Whatever their motivations, enough metropolitan citizens made the move so that small-town population (less than 2,500) actually grew by close to 8 percent in the 1960s. A Census Bureau report of December 1974 showed a net gain to nonmetropolitan areas of 1.8 million persons during the period 1970–74. A government demographer found the assembled statistics to be evidence of an unmistakable reversal of the historic pattern of rural to urban migration.[5] So far as the way of life in the suburbs is concerned, political scientist Robert C. Wood, in his widely respected *Suburbia, Its People and Their Politics,* found that "suburbia is—as a matter of demonstrable fact—the modern carrier of a time-honored and respected ideology," this ideology being that of small-town life and government.[6] In fact, said Wood, what appears to be a mechanized, lock-step life lived in the confines of a massive bureaucracy, is for the commuter a life strongly shaped by the provincial-mindedness of the small town. The point of all this is that rural America can scarcely be called moribund.

In the final analysis, however, what is important is not so much a matter of numbers as it is a matter of cast of mind. What is significant is not the numbers who wish they could live in the country but rather the numbers whose early or late experience of rural living has left a permanent imprint upon their minds. There is an old American saying that you can take the boy out of the country but not the country out of the boy. Even the paraphrased use of this adage by a cigarette manufacturer attests to the well-springs of the American grass-roots psyche which can be tapped with the country-boy approach. Deeply rooted cultural patterns are not easily expunged from the mind. Aside from the definedly rural population of more than fifty million, there are millions upon millions of urbanites and suburbanites who were born to the village and to the sod. Perhaps some of them find a true home in the city, but most of them do not. They sit there in their apartments and provide the nucleus of the national nostalgia for a simpler (and safer) society, a nostalgia manifested by the magnitude of the audience for such television proceedings as *The Waltons* and other more or less pastoral stories.

At a deeper level, what this attachment to "back there"—

whether town, suburban community, or neighborhood—means is that localism is a powerful force in American life. It damns bused integration, damns urban renewal bulldozers, damns big companies that impersonalize life, damns big unions that dictate to locals, damns federal bureaucrats, and generally damns all bigness that negates local allegiances. Veteran sociologist Robert Nisbet, in his *Twilight of Authority,* comments upon localism as a heartfelt part of American life: ". . . the emotional roots of local loyalties remain strong. The results in this country of the government effort to achieve racial balance in the schools is some indication of how profound are human loyalties to neighborhood and local community. I do not doubt that some of the resistance of busing is racist in origins. But by this time agreement is quite general that the greater part of the opposition to such busing springs directly from pride in and sense of attachment to neighborhood." [7] Summarized, grass-roots life in America is, almost by definition, local life, in its several forms.

What is observed here generally is that geographical factors have and have had great shaping power in America. Rural locale especially has operated to produce a mentality clearly distinguishable from that of the born and bred city dweller. It is a mind that had its birth on the farm but was nurtured and brought to its full development in the small-town life of the late nineteenth and early twentieth centuries. It was this mind that came to dominate American culture and politics, this mind that fueled protests against modernism, this mind against which Sinclair Lewis, Sherwood Anderson, and other intellectual zealots fulminated in the 1920s. It is a mind that is pedestrian, unimaginative, and often stolid, a mind with very little grandeur of thought. Perhaps this explains why intellectuals bewailed its dominance and more recently have tried to wish it out of existence. Granville Hicks, who gave a remarkably acute depiction of "Roxborough" in his *Small Town,* makes the point eloquently.

Certain reviewers of *Plainville, U.S.A.* [a study of a typical small Missouri community] were depressed by the picture James West drew of the people in his Ozark town and seemed inclined to dismiss them as sub-human. "Thank God," they said in effect, "most

Americans aren't like this!" My guess is that a large proportion of Americans are a good deal like the people in Plainville and the people in Roxborough, though some of them disguise themselves by wearing city clothes and using city jargon, and most of them manage to keep out of the way of the intellectuals. They are not, by and large, morons or incompetents, but equally they are not at all what the intellectuals think the "common man" ought to be.[8]

Having written the small town out of existence, some intellectuals are mystified when confronted with its continuing reality. In 1970 one of the editors of *Saturday Review,* complaining that "Main Street's uniquely provincial vice lies in its excessive, unquestioning belief (in the Protestant ethic, hard work, honesty, and conventional politics) . . . ," concluded that "Main Street is far away." [9] Yet his essay as a whole provides a convincing testament to the health and vigor of the small town (Mason City, Iowa) that served as the basis of his investigation.

Not only are there such occasional magazine articles of condemnation of the modern small town, but also the visual media frequently presumes its villainy. In any number of contemporary soap operas, melodramas, and films, the city person, portrayed as an innocent foil, is victimized by small-town greed, blackmail, sexual irregularity, political chicanery, hard-line legalism, and assorted subtle dishonesties—in general, by a variety of Peyton Place immoralities. One analyst of such media presentations, remarking that the modern small town of television and certain movies "comes in for a hell of a beating," suggests as a major cause for such vilification the predominantly liberal, ghetto-oriented mentality of script writers. In his view, such script writers, whose entire experience often is urban, see small towns as continuing and active enemies of liberal political ideals, and thus in response portray the town as thoroughly decadent.[9a]

Still, however measured in the contemporary media, the small-town ethos is one of the most interesting cultural creations of the American nineteenth- and twentieth-century experience, having left an indelible imprint on urban attitudes, political practice, hero models, popular culture, and, more generally, on American values. However, as the necessary preface to a detailed summary of this ethos, it must be pointed out that its strongest feature—social-relatedness—is no more than a concentrated essence of a tendency that characterizes grass-roots life wherever found. The small town was what sociologists call a *"Gemeinschaft"* (literally, "community") system, meaning a society characterized by close personal connections between members, along with a valuing of sentiment above individual efficiency. Yet this should not be seen as setting the small town entirely apart from grass-roots life elsewhere. Even if modern urban life may be broadly described as a *"Gesellschaft"* system—a society in which human relations are dominated by *contract,* with individual efficiency being the norm determining retention in the society—the fact is the grass-roots mind characteristically contrives its own *"Gemeinschaft"* system, so to speak, in various ways: it builds strong connectives in its block or neighborhood and in its clubs or corner taverns. It makes family association the crucial experience of day-to-day living. It peoples a personal world with interesting situation comedy or soap opera figures. It demands—and gets—urban newspapers with emphasis on local affairs; significantly, most metropolitan newspapers carry more local news than national and international news combined.[10] The essential point being made here is that the small-town ethos, now to be explored, is but a special manifestation of the grass-roots mind.

### The Small Town's Debt
### to the Farmer

Before examining the main components of the small-town mind, attention must be given to its origins. The American small town owes much to the farmer. He was the reason for its establishment, as the countryside needed supplies and middlemen of various kinds. Especially was this so as the farmer through the course of the nineteenth century became increasingly market-oriented. Trading with and servicing the farmer sustained the small town and gave it enduring agricultural perspectives. From the outset, the townsmen's fortunes rose and fell with those of the farmer, giving rise to intense town interest in weather, crops, and agricultural lore. To be sure, there were antagonisms, centering mostly around the farmer's status as a debtor and taxpayer, but both parties knew that for the most part their political interests coincided. It was a symbiotic relationship, the town for its part contributing services, social opportunities, ideas, and educational facilities. In return the farmer fed the town, drew political attention to it, sustained its merchants, and in a major way contributed to its developing ethos.

The nature of the homesteading process in the nineteenth century made each farm family something of a social unit unto itself. Each initial settlement tract was about a half-mile square, and since the road system was very poor, the farmer had few social contacts. This isolation had a number of effects. It made the family supremely important to its members, to the point where family norms and habits became absolutes. Isolation also accentuated the independence natural to a landholder by forcing the farmer to solve all his physical and technical problems himself, thus generating a sense of resourcefulness that is a foundation stone of individualism. Further, isolation meant that the farmer, and some family members too, spent sixty or seventy hours a week in comparative solitude, essentially companioned only by animals and a demanding environment. This nonverbal existence tended to produce an inward turning and a shyness toward outsiders that some observers have called introversion. To a degree, all of these traits were to become a part of the small-town mentality. But the main impact of isolation was that of heightening what might be called the impulse to community that is a universal human characteristic. Deprived by circumstances of communication beyond the family circle, starved for rich associational relationships with adults of similar interests, the farmer and his wife made the most of every occasion for community relationships. At church socials, at Granger picnics, at harvest balls, the pent-up need to socialize expressed itself. Never mind that weather and crop talk might at last be exhausted, that there are only so many recipes to be exchanged, that the drab hours on the farm had severely narrowed one's outlook—there were always people to talk about, their motives, their secrets, their comings and goings, their peculiarities—these became great subjects of conversation. And when roads improved and communal agricultural neighborhoods formed, or when the railroads fostered community development all along their lines, or when the farmer and his wife retired to the town, the farm-originated habit of intensive social-relatedness deeply influenced community behavior.

Whatever views one holds on the connectives between the ethos of farm life and that of small-community life, it is a certainty that the country and the town have merged in their basic outlook over the past century. Vehicular and road development have made the farmer an active member of some nearby town, as suggested by the fact that when questioned about his geographical location he will almost always give a town identity. Farm life may retain some purely agrarian features, but the farmer is clearly no longer an isolate, and the term "rural" should be understood as reflecting community association and participation.

The farmer and the special circumstances of the small town gave rise to what might be called historically the "small-town mentality." Other terms suggest themselves—the provincial mind, the rural outlook—but these have more of the pejorative flavor of such words as "country bumpkin," "hick," or "hayseed." Even "small-town mentality" has a connotation of backwardness to some, on their assumption that "bigger is better." The view here is that neither the urban nor the rural cast of mind requires an apology—they exist, and if confrontation be the goal it should be sought elsewhere. The term "small-town mentality" represents a conclusion that in the small town a point of view was synthesized that has deeply informed American life. Throughout the approaching pages the past tense will be used, because this is primarily a historical account. Nonetheless, much of what was true remains true. The small-town point of view remains strong; it continues to serve for many millions as the frame of reference according to which day-to-day life is interpreted. For these millions it is the buffer fending off what many call the unpleasant realities of contemporary life.

### Characteristics of the Small-Town Mind

*Social-relatedness*

The small-town mind had several important qualities—a coolness to intellectual abstraction, an indifference to formal religion, a deep-seated individualism—all of these will be discussed. But priority must be given to a very general social-relatedness, because of all things, it dominated the small-town mind.

Life in the small town had something of an organic quality. As a constituent part of the whole each inhabitant was expected to relate strongly to others and to contribute to the companioning that was the essential life principle of the community, thus generating a social whole that was considerably greater than the sum of its parts. As an organic entity the town had an instinct for self-preservation against outsiders. It had a communal memory wherein each person was related to other particular persons, events, neighborhoods, and dates in a highly individual and anecdotal way. Years of childhood, adolescent, and adult exposure to this communal memory gave it continual rebirth and development in individual minds. Town talk struck continually resonating chords in the communal memory, each person's doings seen in the perspective of a wide and rich community experience. As an organic entity the town also had a distinctive environment. It was set well apart from like organisms, and hence generally turned inward, using its own resources for sustaining life and satisfying the social demands of its members. Its lifeblood was the principle of egalitarianism, so powerful that it made the town mighty easily accessible to the town lowly.

The town thus well-served its own. As a known part of a continuing whole, the townsman felt a sense of belonging, and he did belong. Even those whose weakness of character or of the flesh took them out of the mainstream were somehow made to feel a part of the community. This is not to say they were loved. Nor indeed should one say that all the "good" people loved all the other "good" people. The principle of community relations was the principle of association not of affection. Friendship between individuals might develop strongly, but the general community principle was that of association. Not only was there this willingness to associate, but also the townsman was apt to have a wide range of acquaintances. Add to these acquaintances the sometimes extraordinary number of "kinfolk" in the vicinity, and the small towner's human contacts were of much wider range and variety than those of his cousin who had moved to the city.

Generally, then, there was in the small town a rich vein of association, no matter how prosaic its intellectual content. The individual was thus brought close to people, close to the community past, and perhaps because of these very supportive experiences closer and truer to his own inner nature. The small-town resident, as one observer put it, was "tied and stitched into his community in a hundred ways." [11] Despite his frequent irritation at town snoopiness and his periodic resolution to leave these drab surroundings, the small towner was caught in a web, and knew it. A chronicler of American town life expresses this point most effectively:

> For the very closeness of social relationship, and the lack of variety in persons and other objects of attention, which have so many distasteful consequences, are the basis of the profoundest values of small-town life. This is because the formation of deeply rooted sentiments is dependent upon identification with the same objects over a long period of time, and the small town not only encourages but enforces such long-continued identification. In spite of themselves, Minevillers [the locale of this author's research] find themselves developing and holding fond sentiments for the little town they are so prone to abuse. The town takes on somewhat the function of a large family group; it becomes so intimately bound up with the resident's life that for him to reject it is for him to disown a large part of himself. . . . He has grown to demand an intimate community and a particular one—Mineville.[12]

Because of its pettiness there was no living with the small-town culture; but because of its integration into self, there was no living without it.

What might be called the "universal solvent" of small-town life was the quality of neighborliness. Beyond any doubt it was the most esteemed personal attribute one could possess. How highly small towners rated it was suggested in a story by Zona Gale, who was one of the most popular fictional biographers of the early twentieth-century American town. One of the women in "Friendship Village" talks about her town, where "folk have been adventuring together, knowing the details of one another's lives, striving a little but companioning far more than striving, kindling to one another's interests instead of practicing the faint morality of mere civility. . . ." The villagers got together to help out a neighbor, and one of the women says, "I declare, it wasn't so much the stuff they brought, though that was all elegant, but it was the Togetherness of it. I couldn't get to sleep that night for thinkin' about God not havin' anybody to neighbor with." [13] Neighborliness included active assistance of course, but most of all it meant talk. One did not have to be a fluent talker really, but, well, sociable in a number of ways.

One of the manifestations of sociability was a simple willingness to talk. Work could rarely be considered more important than talk—whatever the subject. Avoidance of contact or undue silence was readily interpreted as criticism, and woe be to the person who thus stood apart. This volubility of course included a capacity to linger over commonplaces—the weather, the mail delivery, the newlyweds, the tax deadline, the new road, whatever. Repetitiveness, especially if it were fairly malicious gossip, was not regarded as a fault. Most often the talk centered on simple human facts—births, deaths, partings, returns, etc. Little histories of persons or events, along with anecdotes, punctuated many conversations, activating the communal memory and brightening the conversants' day. Ideas, in the sense of new and fertile conceptions, were a rarity, but the few new conceptions that did somehow catch on were incessantly repeated. In other words, conversational topics, once entering into the mainstream, did not easily wear out. This is understandable, given the recognition that a good part of the communication that went on was aimed not at exchanging information but at reinforcing one's sense of relatedness. Conversational willingness also presumed egalitarian motivations or at least a certain social fearlessness. In exploring waywardness of morals or character one must not be daunted by social distinctions. The mighty as well as the lowly were subject to review. In fact, the higher in the social scale, the more clinical became the details, especially where sex was concerned. Finally, this willingness to converse had to be accompanied by a portion of good judgment: however crimson the distant or recent past of his listener one just did not talk about it, not to his face. Violation of this rule marked one as the worst kind of gossip.

Another social virtue was something that may be called abundance. It helped, that is, to have a good supply of stories and a wealth of enlivening details. In the absence of such riches it was possible, of course, to entertain speculations about some person's motivations (concerning this more later), to add historical perspective to the present subject, or simply to recite a favorite view. Granville Hicks, who observed "Roxborough," found elderly citizens of his town especially comfortable with the tried and locally true:

> . . . constant repetition of the same facts or theories suggests at the very outset that communication in the ordinary sense of the term cannot be the major purpose of these exchanges. An old-timer makes a statement about the soil of Roxborough, for instance, a statement he has made a hundred times to the same listeners, and the listeners respond with the comments they have invariably offered. The old-timer, it seems to me, is talking for the sake of talking—that is, for the sake of establishing a relationship with the group. He is also reaffirming a basic truth, and to him the truth does not have to be novel. Of course people in other walks of life do the same thing, but lawyers and teachers and businessmen sooner or later become aware of the boredom of their audiences. The old-timers are troubled by no such self-consciousness, and so long as they keep to themselves they do not need to be. Their attitude is the exact opposite of the intellectuals, for they are as skeptical of novelty as the intellectuals are devoted to it.[14]

Thus, abundance could take several forms, each of them serving to continue a conversation, but most blessed of all were the prolific local informers, who served as community nerve centers.

Of further assistance to the townsman was an attitude of curiosity. To some extent this came with the small-town package, for lacking the many diversions of city life, local attention was drawn to matters an outsider would consider inconsequential. A Vandalia, Illinois, teacher put it this way: "People here are interested in what other people are up to, not in what they think." [15] But this curiosity was not simply a matter of avid interest in anything deviating from routine; it included an acute inquisitiveness into the motives of other people. It is not too much to say that the favorite community pastime was speculation in motives. The usual presumption was that people did things out of spite, or because of some private and quite personal distress. In either case, causality could be fairly well-established because townsmen knew each other's emotional background so well. Of especial attractiveness in a gossip gathering was the shrewd analyst who could discern reverberations in a current insult of an unkind cut of perhaps five years back. Such explorations in motivation constituted outrageous invasions of privacy, but small towners knew it and joked about it. It drove some people out, but the ones who stayed, further to explore motivation, became the keenest amateur psychologists this country ever produced. The townsman knew more people than did his city cousin; he knew more character types along with their variations of intellect, temperament, and attainments; he knew them more intimately and in a greater variety of situations. Small wonder that he achieved near maximum development as a social observer.

Neighborliness extended much further than talk. In times of personal crisis—death, sickness, economic emergency—many helping hands reached out and made sure the necessities of life were provided. Sometimes this was institutionalized through churches, service organizations, or "sunshine committees." Whichever the case, for the time being old grudges were forgotten. Neighborly assistance was also provided for temporary needs, as for food, tools, utensils, and the like. There was much lending back and forth, but with this kind of assistance it was advisable to keep some informal account of favors owed to others and due from them. Otherwise one ran the risk of being labeled as a "bad borrower." James West, in *Plainville, U.S.A.*, recounts one such experience, illuminating both the attitude toward borrowing and the indirect style of the small towner:

> One old woman told me of her "last bad borrier." A younger woman kept borrowing a fruit jar full of flour and returning it not quite full of poorer flour. "So I fixed her. I kept that fruit jar just for her. When she brought it back with less flour than she took, I set it on the shelf for next time. Finally it didn't have no flour in it. But when she come to borry I handed it to her just the same and

said, "This is *your* flour." So then she seen what I meant, and she ain't never been back.[16]

Neighborliness was woven into the fabric of community, but for all the symmetry of its exterior pattern, the underside of the fabric was much less attractive. There is a substantial amount of human meanness in all communities, and its presence was unmistakable in the small town, most notably in gossip. Greatly informative in this connection is the analysis of "people talk" in "Springdale, N.Y." by Arthur Vidich and Joseph Bensman. The authors found there are two levels of communication. At the public level, conversation about people included only the "good things about people —'a man who has always done good things for the town'; 'a swell guy'; 'she's always doing good things for people'; 'a person who never asks anything in return.' More than this the level of public conversation always focused on the collective success of the community and the individual successes of its members." At the private level, however (and this is the level of gossip), a considerable amount of carving is done, but only in "small temporarily closed circles" and only on those who are not present. However vicious, the gossip does not unduly disturb the public level of conversation:

> . . . it is true that everyone knows everything about everyone else but, because of the way the information is learned, it does not ordinarily affect the everyday interpersonal relations of people; in public view even enemies speak to each other. When the victim meets the gossiper, he does not see him as a gossip and the gossiper does not let the privately gained information affect his public gestures; both greet each other in a friendly and neighborly manner and, perhaps, talk about someone else.[17]

So much for the mechanics of gossip. But its anatomy requires further description. It was not endemic to the small towner to be more interested in peculiarities than in virtue, and more interested in vice than in peculiarities. What did set him apart was his milieu, in which frequency of contact greatly increased the likelihood of abrasions from personality conflicts. Further, his limited perspective caused him to focus more intensively on any local insults, somewhat in the fashion of photographic enlargements. Rivalries in business, in politics, in love, or otherwise brought tendencies toward ruthless evaluation of others. Subtle or even imagined affronts provoked responses of equal severity, so that the townsman lived in "a world of mysterious grudges and unspoken grievances." In such a climate nobody could escape unscathed. Sometimes the spite was ungovernable and required a daily lancing of one's enemy; more often an occasional pinking would do, perhaps only by tone of voice.

Undoubtedly gossip served as a more effective social policeman than did the Ten Commandments. In Vandalia, Illinois, for example, a researcher found that the town's "social and moral regularity depends greatly on several thousand pairs of eyes. . . . In a town where the lives of their neighbors are the yarn of everyone's knitting, it is possible to be immoral, but utterly past imagination that one remain undetected." [18] In *Hoosier Village* Newell Sims found that "Personal conduct is freely discussed. . . . The rumors set afloat by gossips are usually accepted as true by the great majority, and the community never forgets. . . . It is not too much to say that in the village, gossip plays the part of an invisible policeman." [19] Under the circumstances there were many whose inclinations were bent back into socially acceptable channels. The tenor of town interest in wayward behavior was only infrequently that of moral censure. Perhaps this was because despite its reputation (and with some exceptions), small-town America was not a religious people—churchly, maybe, but not religious (see page 83). Private sins and public scandals were seen with something of an amused tolerance, a tolerance no doubt bred by a considerable appreciation of human weakness. Anyone who daily lives—who has to live—with a sprinkling of adulterers, drunkards, and wife-beaters, sees more the forest of human failings than the single trees of human corruption. If the people of the city assumed sanctimonious airs about all this, they were reminded that their daily newspapers often went one degree further by their willingness to print what small towners were discreet enough to keep among themselves.

The social-relatedness of the small town was intensified by something the townsman had learned from the farmer: the importance of family. Family tradition was strong, and role definitions (father, mother, child) unquestioned—this in itself a powerful source of security. Kinfolk relations were spread throughout the community. This extended family was essentially the first line of one's defense, and though its guiding theme was as often tolerance as affection, emotional ties were such that "family" was a sufficient password to assure meals and lodging when necessary. As the young matured and eased away from a strictly family network, they were increasingly fastened into a community network by being personally recognized in the community, by engagement in community athletic events, or by a sense of exclusivity fostered when townsmen talked ungraciously of "outsiders." Most certainly community attachment was furthered by a defensiveness felt when city people mocked the unsophisticated rural style. The chronology of development of community attachment was such that by early adolescence the young boy or girl had clear feelings of identification that were not easy to eradicate. Even when the young man or woman left, town memories endured, as an Iowa wanderer observed: ". . . migrant natives never forget a corner of town or any people. However much they speak of glories elsewhere—they're always homesick." [20] The town had become a part of one's thinking, and this far more integrally than the contrived boosterism that characterizes chambers of commerce. It was an attractively reciprocal arrangement—for its part the town receiving an addition to its lifeblood of social-relatedness, and for his part the individual receiving the satisfaction of integration into a whole, as well as perhaps the greatest blessing of all, that sense of living within a familiar and manageable world.

With American society as mobile as it was, the town had frequent relations with "outsiders," both transient people and newly permanent residents. It was an uneasy confrontation—not really an unfriendliness on the town's part, but something of an arm's length relationship. Perhaps this was a legacy of the "old days," when it was burden enough to care for the community's ill and incapacitated without an unproductive drifter adding to the burden. Perhaps it was the implicit threat that a stranger represented to the stable routine of the town. More likely it was the influence of the community's "inner life," which, with its shared confidences, appreciation of idiosyncrasies, and easy allusions, made it impenetrable to outsiders for a long, long time. A newcomer simply had to ask too many questions, his questions themselves a mark of his foreignness. Indeed, it is doubtful that he could ever be fully accepted: one Roxborough local put it this way: "You can't become a naturalized citizen in less than a century." Certainly no outsider could hope to make significant changes in the town's way of living.

City people were periodic visitors to the small town and often found it an uncomfortable experience. The battle between the country and the city has gone on for a long time. More than two thousand years ago the Roman poet Horace complained of Rome's crowds, intrigues, and empty friendships, asking himself, "O rural home, how soon shall I see you again?" In America the battle was joined early and has continued sporadically through the present century. Small towners have been acutely aware of the contemptuous terms city dwellers used to describe them—hick, hayseed, rube, and the like.* Such descriptions produced feelings of inferiority, which were accentuated in personal contacts with city people, who spoke faster, in wider perspectives, and in a more versatile idiom than they could themselves. But the reaction of inferiority was a shallow one, for the country people stoutly believed their way of life superior, however socially awkward they might feel in their urban contacts.

As the townsman contrasted it with rural life, the city was saturated with violence and crime; it was victimized by unscrupulous labor leaders with collectivistic attitudes; it was unwholesome for children; it bred loneliness and immorality; it was excessively competitive; its schools fostered dangerous and un-American "isms"; its populations were suspect, being unduly numerous in olive-skinned newcomers. This antagonism to the city had other ramifications. One student of American prejudice found a residual anti-Semitism in America to have its source in such

---

* Nor has the abuse stopped. In 1971 a *New York Times* reporter visiting Pontiac, Illinois, unflatteringly described Main Street as a "symbol of self-satisfied provincialism and narrow boosterism." See also p. 63.

opposition. Though Jews might be wholly unknown in the small town, still they represented a people who adapted readily to city life, and even rose to control some aspects of it. Thus they became an integral part of the vague urban complex seen as the enemy.[21]

The foregoing list by no means exhausts the catalogue of urban evils, but it is indicative of the town's understanding of city life. However, the city was not rejected in every way. It was too useful—in its economic relations, in its job opportunities, and for its shopping and entertainment attractions. In essence, what the country took from the city was the machine, and this it took enthusiastically. The machine in all of its forms, for work and for home, sharply upgraded town life. Most of all the townsmen welcomed the automobile, which enabled them to use the city, but not to have to put up with it. This attitude may be summarized by saying that rural America embraced the machine, but not machine civilization.

The social-relatedness of the town can be seen to encompass a wide spectrum of individual behavior and attitude and of community practice. From one point of view, this complex may be called "narrow" and "provincial." From another it may be seen as the best circumstance for the "decent development of the human being as a social animal."

*Intellectual Features*

For all of its neighborly warmth and unaffected charm, the small-town mind was not a particularly flexible instrument. It was rarely taxed by the demands made upon it; furthermore, the pace of such demands as there were permitted a leisurely mode of thought. The kinds of problems with which it dealt were practical in nature and fairly commonplace, so theorizing as a constant mental practice was unnecessary. Moreover, as developed earlier, the social-relatedness of town life brought a stream of thought that was highly "peopled"—in the sense that people were the usual stopping points on the mental track. The general consequence of these influences was a mind which, however insightful and imaginative, lacked concentrative powers and logical efficiency. It was not a disorderly mind by any means, but a mind that tended to use fewer categories by which experience is understood—excepting, of course, in its comprehension of people.

A number of traits followed from the basic limitations just described. One of the most important of them was that lacking in speculative development, the small towner tended to accept ideas given him by one of the several sources of his tradition. He was apt to believe in some of the old wives' tales—"to make dogs fierce, feed gunpowder to them"; "to grow good peppers, get mad when planting them"; "rainwater caught on the first of June serves as a cure for freckles." He was frequently superstitious. He trusted in "folk wisdom"—aphoristic sayings of the Benjamin Franklin variety: "Haste makes waste." He was likely to be a primitivist, regarding more favorably instinctual impulse, or intuition, or "inner light," than intellectual refinement. Almost certainly he did not hold in high esteem intellectual sophistication—precisely the feature upon which so many city people prided themselves. Though not necessarily hostile to new ideas, the townsman was usually uncomfortable with them, especially when patronizingly expressed by visiting city dwellers. Trusting in the "tried and true" rather than the theoretical, he wanted his schools to give maximum attention to practical affairs. People, and the personal word rather than printed matter, were the prime source of education.

Another notable trait of the small-town mentality was its obliqueness. In social discourse where issues were divisive, or where confrontation was likely to be embarrassing, the townsman tended to be circumlocutory. He talked around the issue, past it, in indirect reference to it, or otherwise dealt with it in a vague but somehow effective way. Such indirection of approach is illustrated by an incident recorded by Granville Hicks in *Small Town:*

One day an old-timer told me about the house he had bought in New York City when he worked there. "It was a two-family house, and after we came back here, we let half of it to a sort of cousin. He was supposed to collect the rent for the other half and take care of the repairs, and he got his rent free. Well, he didn't send me any money, and after a while I found that he hadn't even paid the taxes." "I bet you made it hot for him," I said. The old-timer smiled slyly. "I made up my mind that I wasn't going to put up with that, so I sold the house, and he didn't know a thing about it till he got his orders to get out." [22]

Whether such obliqueness was traceable to the townsman's discomfort with the rigors of argument, or to his highly developed sensitivity to others in face-to-face meetings is moot. But strangers soon learned that the townsman's offhand ways were often the mask for a deadly serious intent.

What has been said about the mental traits of the small towner should not obscure the fact that high intelligence was as widely distributed in the town as it was in the city. But because it often was manifested in distinctly practical ways, it gave a different impression. Applied to a practical problem it emerged as inventiveness or ingenuity; directed to human problems it was sage and discerning rather than analytical; channeled into business affairs it showed itself as shrewdness and agility; applied to abstruse discussion (whether printed or oral) it revealed itself as commonsensical; exercised in day-to-day conversation it disclosed gifts of description and narration. Lacking in aesthetic sensitivity, in affluence of conception, and in elegance of language, the most acute townsmen manifested their intellectual riches in depth of human understanding, in quickness of insight, and in the ability accurately to read a present situation.

Perhaps the small-town mind can best be comprehended by an appreciation of its encounter with the intellectuals.* Hostilities between the town and the intellectual commenced a long time back in American history, at least as far back as 1635, when free-thinker Roger Williams was expelled from the Massachusetts Bay colony. Intermittent warfare continued through the eighteenth and nineteenth centuries and reached its climax in the 1920s with the feverish denunciations of small-town America by de-

---

* The meaning of "intellectual" as here used follows that of Richard Hofstadter in *Anti-Intellectualism in American Life*. While generally the "briefcase carrying professions—lawyers, engineers, doctors—may be called intellectuals, they live '*off*' ideas, not for them." Those who in some sense live for them—teachers, artists, writers—is the intended usage here.

racinated intellectuals of the postwar period. But for its part small-town America never issued a major excommunication against them. Intellectuals had their usefulness, becoming suspect only when they exceeded their role, and becoming anathema only when they decisively violated it.

In the town's eyes the intellectual functioned as a supplier of tools, a purveyor of the cultural tradition, and possibly an agency of entertainment. Through the teaching staff of the local school the young were to be provided the basic skills of reading, writing, and figuring. Along with these skills it was expected that students should be brought to understand the ideas, events, and persons that together formulated American values and its political heritage. It was not necessary for the teacher to voice explicit endorsement of the moral virtues, but neither was it allowable to raise questions, directly or indirectly, about their validity. It was perfectly acceptable to range into poetry, novels, and drama—in fact, assuming that the excursions were relatively harmless, such explorations were entertaining and might breed a mature literary taste in those who went in for that sort of thing. In general then, in areas where tradition and morals were involved, the teacher was to function as a parental surrogate. All of this necessary verbal acculturation was to be supplemented with substantial opportunities to learn technical and practical skills and sports skills too. At the highest levels of education, college and graduate school teachers had the responsibility of continuing the training regimen, returning to the world graduates who were occupationally and professionally qualified. Most decidedly it was not their responsibility to tamper with either the student's moral framework or his ideological commitment.

For the duration of the nineteenth century and a few years of the twentieth the intellectual fulfilled the townsman's trust, but then he began to fail it, and soon failed it badly. The world of the intellectual is a verbal or symbolic world through which he ranges in search of what he perceives to be truth. This symbolic world relates to the concrete world, even explains it to a degree, but its limits are far wider, and its possibilities limited only by imaginal power. From a mundane standpoint, explorations in this symbolic world have several dangers, some of them perhaps minor, but several that are major, at least from the townsman's point of view.

Concerning the minor dangers, one of the penalties of excessive concern with the ideational world rather than the real world is that the explorer becomes nonfunctional. He engages in verbal play, creating wordy pyrotechnics, disputing for the sake of disputing, doing mental gymnastics. Further, indiscriminate junketing in the symbolic world is liable to result in extremes of subjectivism. The small towner yielded to few in his devotion to traditional American individualism, and it was allowable to hear and march to the tune of a different drummer—but not to the ridiculous point where one's stream of consciousness was allowed exclusively to dictate the content of canvas or manuscript. At very best, preoccupation with the symbolic world resulted in knowledge for knowledge's sake alone, producing a set of dry facts of little use to anybody. Provincial bafflement at such inquiries was recorded by a Roxborough native:

> There is a summer visitor who every year sets himself a task in nature study. One year mushrooms occupied his attention, and sometimes Mr. Cutter accompanied him on long trips to gather specimens. An account of these expeditions became part of Mr. Cutter's long saga on the eccentricities of the visitor, and one day I heard it at the store. It was a good story, too, with gestures of poking here and there, a back bent under a heavy load, expressions of chagrin and triumph as the specimens were examined. It came to a climax: "He doesn't eat 'em; he doesn't even like 'em."

The conventional small towner could not see much point in expending a lot of effort for remote facts. Nonetheless, such studies were harmless, and thus tolerable, just as it was tolerable to accept the intellectuals' statement that "there are two sides to every question," even though the townsman according to his own lights would modify the statement.

It probably did not make any difference to the occasional intellectual that "happened" into town, but there was further peril in venturing into the world of ideas. It made a person unfit to live with. At best he became a comic Ichabod; at worst he was a menacing subversive. Given town social ideals, few intellectuals were brought to its bosom. The intellectual was a bookworm and rarely seen. When he was seen he had an ungainly look about him that somehow didn't fit in. When he engaged in conversation he was known to have embarrassed his company by the language of theory rather than the language of fact. There were too many long pauses in the conversation. Too often he fell silent; and, what kind of sneering thoughts was he thinking anyway? He seemed to befriend ideas instead of people. He couldn't seem to relax and be loud and let himself go. It was rumored that his morals were not what they should be. It was likely that he lacked red corpuscles, and who knows where that might lead?

If the intellectual's offenses, real and imagined, were only those so far detailed, the town would simply have had no truck with him and let it go at that. But as said earlier, the intellectual failed the town's trust *badly*. In ranging through the symbolic world it is very possible for an intellectual to fall in love with certain ideals or conceptions sharply different from those prevailing in the real world. Such affection is innocent enough if the ideals in question relate to poetic practices, historical patterns, or other matters of remote general significance. In such cases, eccentricities are readily excused. However, where the intellectual's ardor becomes attached to political or social ideals very different from those by which society is currently governed, he becomes a threat. Even more does he become a threat when he espouses a view of human nature deeply variant from that of the intuitive mind.

In the townsman's view it was not simply that the intellectual had gone beyond his defined role as understood in the local mind. Nor was it simply that too many intellectuals made a pretense of educating while in fact indoctrinating. Nor was it that reform, which, typically, intellectuals advocated, was necessarily undesirable. The townsman's hostility to the intellectual rested, at last, on an intuition that his view of human nature was warped, skewed badly to the rational side, and almost wholly ignorant of the emotional side, and the organic side. Brilliant, scholarly, logical, eloquent, knowledgeable—these were the intellectual's credentials. But they were not enough, not nearly. The town rested in the intuition that there is in each human being a mysterious inner world, a world painstakingly pieced together out of experience, love, logic, and relationship with others. It is composed of basal truths and provides the essential network within which day-to-day existence is carried on. It has its own processes, which are a bit different with each individual, its own secrets, its own private proclivities to evil. Generally, this town view of human nature regards life as an essentially integrative process, wherein remodeling and replacing is the theme, rather than destroying and rebuilding. But of this the intellectual understood little. However wide were his venturings in the symbolic world, however extensive his knowledge, he was insensitive to the fundamental subtlety of human nature. He was peculiarly deficient, in the town view—huge blocks of knowledge, but little of the mortar of understanding. And, intuitively, townsmen thought it folly to entrust the young to this type of ignorance. Their intuition was confirmed in fact when the town sons and daughters came home from the university to deny and ridicule town precepts.

Under the influence of twentieth-century relativistic philosophies, the intellectual had little respect for the town's conception of human nature, even if he had understood it, which was rarely. But he did know what should be done with young minds. His task was to free them from all forms of what he called "cant," from faith, from moral imperatives, from fixed principles, from "unscientific knowledge," from natural law. With wit, jargon, and eloquence he set about dismantling the fragile inner worlds of his students, disintegrating the anchor truths so laboriously put together. The mind should be completely open, that was the ideal. With confidence he projected a new world shaped from his abstract venturings. But then the class bell rang, and the student was left alone to piece together a decent and warmly human world out of the jargon and abstruse theory that had been provided. He often failed, and naked before reality, he accepted any system of ideas that promised an orderly existence, no matter how exotic its components. At last, the more sensitive of the intellectuals were now ready to grant what the townsman thought he knew all along: that education presumes a respect for priorities of the human heart, and its axioms should not be made the subject of the educator's value judgment.

Its estrangement from the intellectuals reveals a lot about the small-town mentality—its simplicity, its practicality, its lack of sophistication, its suspicion, its limited breadth, its tendency to the concrete, its accusative nature, its genuine warmth of inclination, its mysticism. Indeed, its major patterns are epitomized by the clash. However, to complete the story, other features require exploration.

## Religious Characteristics

To many Americans in the cities the small town carried the reputation of being strongly religious. If by this is meant church attendance, the reputation may have been deserved. But if by "strongly religious" is meant piety, the pervasive integration of religion into day-to-day life, the reputation is unmerited. Observers of the American small town have been unimpressed with the natives' dedication to the life of the spirit. Moderate conformance to moral stricture there was, but the sanction was far more reliant upon the threat of adverse gossip than upon religious scruple.

The lack of piety was most strongly evident in Protestant denominations, though there were exceptions, as will be noted. In Roxborough, Granville Hicks found little interest in dogma, a notable indifference to religion as an institution, and a "bewildered latitudinarianism" as to moral principle. In Mineville townspeople showed little interest in church. Excluding Catholics, whose church attendance was regular, 90 percent of the citizenry were "frankly indifferent and rarely if ever enter the church door." Springdale Protestants were churchgoers, but for them theology, while a part of churchly rhetoric, was a negligible consideration (except for Baptists). It did not materially shape their essential views or attitudes, so that for them religion meant "an added layer of social activity which merely thickens the public life of the four hundred people out of about 2,500 population who participate." In Plainville, James West found religious interest to be very low, and though the natives did pay heed to the moral standards espoused by the churches, the coercive force was fear of gossip. A study of Vandalia yielded a conclusion of predominant Protestant apathy (again, excepting Baptists), with one Lutheran minister complaining that the Protestant church "spends most of its time adding a mellifluous odor to the prevailing winds." In general the tendencies toward weakening dogma and declining moral forcefulness of the small-town churches have been accompanied by heightened participation in community organizations and service projects. In his recent study of the town in American history, Page Smith summarizes these developments most clearly:

> The Protestant churches of the town (except perhaps in the South) are hardly distinguishable from those of the city. Liberal in theology and "social" in polity, they are less concerned with producing saints than good citizens. . . . Its members are encouraged to seek in the church "a partnership with God," which, they are told, will help business, remove anxiety, lower blood pressure, and make America strong; the church offers them "a life with meaning," but, it is to be feared, one without the deeper commitment of faith and without moral grandeur.[23]

If the early rapport between the small town and Christian religion has been breached in the twentieth century, there has remained an underlying spirit with strong religious overtones. The small town had a legacy from its farmer forebears of an encounter with nature, an experience that bred certain quasi-religious attitudes. The townsman had an easy relatedness to all forms of life, a resignation in the face of powerful forces, a fatalism in the face of natural processes. He had not quite the farmer's fear of nature's awesome power, but retained a trained respect for its vicissitudes. From these attitudes emerged a certain personal humility that is at the foundation of all religion. On the light side this brought the reluctance to tamper with nature exhibited by a Roxborough stock-raiser, who, when questioned by his wife as to how the cows took to daylight-saving time during its first few days of usage in World War II, said, "They wanted to know who that damned fool was waking 'em up in the middle of the night." On the serious side it expressed itself in preoccupation with nature. The town immersed itself in it. The weather and the status of the crops were always major conversational topics. Hunting and fishing were important elements of each townsman's youth, and as a city dweller in adult years, he awaited the day of the season's opening. Inevitably, comparisons between city and town living concluded on a note of the town's advantage of being close to nature in the raw. In summary, nearly every small towner, placed and displaced, would agree with the saying that God made the country and man made the city.

## Provincial Individualism

It was mentioned earlier that one of the features of city life most objectionable to the townsman was the apparent collectivism it implied. This assessment may have been wildly in error, but when he saw large-scale organizations and city masses it affronted his deep-dyed individualism. In this attitude he reflected the rural environment, which had long demanded that an individual be capable of doing pretty nearly everything for himself as the price of continued existence in the country. From this a kind of "can do" attitude emerged, which made for a general sense of being able to manage one's own affairs. Further, the small towner had always been relatively free of institutionalized pressure. He could work at his own pace and rarely was he subjected to the routinization of his efforts. Nor was he plagued by bureaucratic rules. He could easily "take off" an afternoon if the weather and the hunting prospects warranted it. The townsman became self-confident and independent, sometimes brashly so, suffering subordination with ill-humor. Thus was an already strong American egalitarianism deepened.

Because it was a root principle, provincial individualism notably influenced attitudes on various matters. Personal and real property were held sacred, this meaning, among other things, that the small town most often sided with management in its controversies with labor unions. Besides, the latter fully exemplified the collective principle that was anathema to the townsman. Individualism also shaped the town outlook on the law. While the necessity for law was understood, the attitude toward its local enforcement was very negative. This view extended from game laws (regarded as "city laws" aimed at providing sport for urban dwellers) to such felonies as misappropriation of government funds. In fact, the general expectation was that one went into government for the same reason he went into anything else—to make plenty if possible. The matter of politicians' "cutting a fat hog" at public expense occasioned little surprise, possibly because the natives viewed government essentially as an adversary. In Mineville the town's most respectable citizens were "likely to joke about breaking important laws and not be affected adversely by public pressure." In Plainville, state and federal law was "dreaded and even hated." In Roxborough, Hicks found the same pattern:

> . . . every predatory pioneer instinct goes into operation when the average native is confronted with his government—town, state, or federal. Governmental bodies apparently exist to be cheated, and regulations were made to be evaded. It is no wonder that during the war the black market had its Roxborough customers. Many of those who bought in the black market were intensely patriotic, and not merely in words, but they followed their deepest convictions and got theirs when and where the getting was good. The fact that in getting theirs they were putting something over on the government did not diminish their pleasure.[24]

Given such negative views toward government it is evident that the townsman's strong sense of community described earlier was directed to people, not to government.

Any summary of American small-town mentality must highlight that special balance of individualism and collectivism that prevailed there. The collectivism of the town was of a wide-mesh type. Townspeople were caught up in a net of certain standard attitudes and behavioral expectations, and social pressure operated potently to keep them enmeshed. Yet, paradoxically, the network gave powerful support to the principle of individualism. Its widely spaced openings permitted great eccentricities of personality to develop. In fact, the town ethos in a way encouraged such idiosyncratic development. Where ideas are scarce, talk is much enhanced by such variations of personal temperament as cast a different light on common conversational topics. Most of all, the town network assured personal acceptance. Day after day and at every point, the townsman's human craving for recognition as a person was satisfied. Anchored by this acceptance he could fully express his inclinations, with a consequent deepening and enrichment of the emotional patterns of his temperament. If this brought with it a certain grossness that city people found distasteful, it brought also a fullness of development of personality, a kind of personal individualism that gave the townsman both dignity and style.

In the richness and in the poverty of the American small town was formed much of what has come to be called the American character. The small town has stood, and still stands, for what is most American about Americans. It is not surprising that, as one historian put it, concern with the town—in its richness and its poverty—has "pre-empted the greater part of our literature." [25] And of the literature that remains, much is concerned with the South. It is to that geographical mentality that this exploration will now turn.

## THE SOUTHERN VARIANT OF
## THE SMALL-TOWN MIND

In William Faulkner's *Absalom, Absalom!* the young Quentin Compson has just told his college roommate the history of Thomas Sutpen and others of that tragic Mississippi family. His roommate, who is from Canada, responds:

> "I just want to understand it [the peculiarities of the Southern mind] if I can and I don't know how to say it better. Because it's something my people haven't got. Or if we have got it, it all happened long ago across the water and so now there ain't anything to look at every day to remind us of it. We don't live among defeated grandfathers and freed slaves (or have I got it backward and was it your folks that are free and the niggers that lost?) and bullets in the dining room table and such, to be always reminding us to never forget. What is it? something you live and breathe in like air? a kind of vacuum filled with wraithlike and indomitable anger and pride and glory at and in happenings that occurred and ceased fifty years ago? a kind of entailed birthright father and son and father and son of never forgiving General Sherman, so that forevermore as long as your children's children produce children you wont be anything but a descendant of a long line of colonels killed in Pickett's charge at Manassas?"

"Gettysburg," Quentin said. "You cant understand it. You would have to be born there." [26]

In a figurative sense a South was born that July third of 1863 at Gettysburg, a South of boldness, of courage, of rolling drums, of rebel yells, of magnificent leadership. It was a South that a legion of writers and poets would make forever memorable, creating a collected imagery that would linger warmly in a people's imagination through generations of time. In an asphalt age, it would continue as an imaginal reservoir, informing a people's values and distinguishing a people's history. In sum, what was born at Gettysburg was an idea of great captivating power.

As Alexis de Tocqueville mused a century and a half ago, maintenance of a distinct cultural identity in America is no easy task. The tyranny of the majority reaches into every corner of life, bending and shaping everything to its own *Weltanschauung*. The American national motto, E Pluribus Unum—literally "one out of many"—itself reflects this cultural impetus, as does the turn of mind that insists that immigrants merge themselves totally into the American social environment. All those who continue to indulge cultural diversity are, in the words of one observer, urged to go and "baptize themselves in the national mainstream." But somehow (and the social mechanics of it *are* uncertain) the South has maintained its uniqueness. There are views to the contrary, of course, and a wealth of popular literature describes a "changed" South, a "new" South, an "indistinguishable" South: opinions are offered that a Southerner may now be comfortable almost anywhere in the country and vice versa. Yet sensitive, insistent voices—novelists, historians, essayists—have continued to describe a region where the sound and flavor and feel of experience are different. Quite recently (1972) a sociologist, John Shelton Reed, undertook a scientific study to test the validity of such continuing appraisals. In his work *The Enduring South* he concluded that they were—right. On the basis of extensive sociological evidence he found that Southerners are more religious, more attached to home and place, more violent than non-Southerners —in all, significantly different from them.[27] His findings include the urban South. No, the South stands apart from the American mainstream. It has a mind of its own. It has a special quality not duplicated elsewhere in America, but there are features it shares with other grass-roots Americans, notably those of the small town.

It has been mentioned that the small town's encounter with nature significantly influenced its basic perspective. The same is equally to be said of the South. Somewhere in his works Robert Frost said of Americans "The land was ours before we were the land's." [28] The tempo at which a land works its way into the hearts and minds of its inhabitants remains a mystery, but somehow it happened to Southerners long before it happened to the rest of America. It helped, too, that much of the South has unusual natural beauty, which, according to historian W. J. Cash, conspires in favor of romance:

> The country is one of extravagant colors, of proliferating foliage and bloom, of flooding yellow sunlight, and, above all perhaps, of haze. Pale blue fogs hang above the valleys in the morning, the atmosphere smokes faintly at midday, and through the long slow afternoon cloud-stacks tower from the horizon and the earth-heat quivers upward through the iridescent air, blurring every outline and rendering every object vague and problematical. . . .
>
> The dominant mood, the mood that lingers in the memory, is one of well-nigh drunken reverie—of a hush that seems all the deeper for the far-away mourning of the hounds and the far-away crying of the doves—of such sweet and inexorable opiates as the rich odors of hot earth and pinewood and the perfume of the magnolia in bloom. . . . [29]

And it helped that the South fought the invader across its land, consecrating it with the blood of its young men. So it happened that the land burned its way into the mind of the Southerner. And the youthful days of quail hunting, of upland hiking, and of sun drowsing gave him concrete experience, which in later years, and perhaps far from home, added nostalgia to an already rich imagery of the land.

If small-town neighborliness was often layered over with back-biting and a bit of surliness toward outsiders, the Southern variety was mellower and less insistent on a gossip principle. The rhythms of Southern life were slower, perhaps because of the climate necessarily so. Nor was the Southerner a devotee of the work ethic so common to the American mind generally. He had time on his hands, which in the view of one Southern observer, is "the first requirement of neighborliness . . . it allows for the idiosyncrasies of actual people." [30] He had more time for people, and along with it, a relaxed and easygoing manner that nourished companionable exchanges. Further, a lingering aristocratic tradition, which emphasized manners and courtesy, enabled an easy avoidance of temperamental clashes. Generally, then, the neighborliness of the South had a different feel and texture than that of the northern small town.

Other influences further distinguished the social life of the South. As a farm and small-town people Southerners had the same social closeness described earlier, but were even more intensely organic than was the case elsewhere. For one thing, Southerners were an inbred people. Few immigrants came south; nor have Southerners been a mobile people. As a consequence, Southerners have tended to marry within the South, with the resultant buildup of cousins of various degrees and in-laws of indirect connection. Though few kept lineage charts, there was an at least latent and very often real sense of belonging as one found that he had an identity even several hundred miles away within the South. Further intensifying the Southern sense of relatedness was a quality that may be described as an emphasis upon the personal. Several careful observers of the South have commented upon this: W. J. Cash saw Southerners as "simple, direct, and immensely personal"; James McBride Dabbs viewed them as devotees to the "cult of persons," which might include anyone from General Robert E. Lee down to and including the village drunk—a man is important simply because he is a man; historian David Potter credited the South with being a major author of "personalism," which gave life a meaning and a relatedness, which "our more bountiful life in the mass culture" seemed to lack.[31] The organic principle is essentially a matter of relatedness. This principle was only furthered by Southern kinship ties and emphasis upon the personal.

A provincial individualism of the small town was more than matched by the unrestrained variety characteristic of the Southerner. In one analyst's view, the Southerner's was "the most intense individualism the world has seen since the Italian Renaissance and its men of 'terrible fury.' "[32] The fierce Celtic temperament that predominated among early Southern settlers resisted authoritarian domination in America, just as it had in Ireland and Scotland. And this querulous nature was not softened by infusion of more sedate blood, as the waves of nineteenth-century immigration bypassed a slave-conscious South. The frontier experience gave the freest possible rein to this temperamental individualist, making him something of a law unto himself. With the development of the plantation system, individualism was crystallized into an ethos for generations to come. The plantation functioned as a self-contained unit (except for produce marketing), and as members of the political leadership, the planters made sure their domains were not unduly interfered with by law and government. By the time of the Civil War, this individualism manifested itself at the grass-roots level by the willingness of the Confederate soldier "to jeer openly and unabashed in the face of Stonewall Jackson when that austere Presbyterian captain rode along his lines." In the late nineteenth and early twentieth centuries that individualism was reflected by effective circumvention of federal laws relating to the Negro. That it continues to be powerfully operative is suggested by continuing Southern grass-roots resistance to big government of whatever form.

A Southern society that was intensely organic could tolerate the strong individualism of the Southerner because it was an individualism which, however much it resisted external restraints, was continually cognizant of other people—as individuals. What it could not tolerate was excessive disturbance of the established dependencies and relations prevailing among the social members. New ways of thought, speculations about the existing order, theorizing about social principles—such intellectual adventuring could lead to "isms" that would poison the social organism. Indeed, having suffered at the hands of one "ism"—abolitionism—the South resisted all abstractions, aware of their disintegrating power. One Southerner put it this way: "Your Southerner is typically a realist. He will embrace practically anything life brings if it comes without benefit of theory; but if it comes waving a banner he is almost certain to grab his sword and, without further consideration, have at it." [33] Pursuit of abstractions, whether they be "civil rights" or "women's rights" or "students' rights" or whatever, usually winds up violating what Robert Penn Warren called "the massiveness of experience, the concreteness of life." For this reason the Southerner has leaned, historically, to the traditional and the structured. As recently as the early 1970s he continued to do so, as the studies of political scientist Daniel Elazar have shown.[34]

From what has been said over the past few pages it is clear that the grass-roots South has, with some variations, several of the same patterns of thought and action that characterize small-town America. A Midwesterner could feel at home there, perhaps. Time would gradually soften his hard "r's" and slow his speech cadences. Experience would slacken his concern with work in favor of leisure. Association would slowly color his manners to a Southern style. Marriages would elaborate his kinship connections. Yet with all of these changes the Midwesterner would remain a stranger in a strange land, for he would not have carried what historian C. Vann Woodward has called "the burden of Southern history." He would not have shared in the collective experience of the Southern people.

One of the most powerful and compelling themes of American history is that of her super-eminence among the nations of the earth over the past two centuries. The country has stood for praiseworthy ideals; it has succored nations in distress; and it has won every war it seriously pursued. Because their history is studded with victory, Americans have woven into the very texture of their minds an optimism and high expectation concerning the purposes and goals of their nation. As Americans, Southerners share in this ideology of American greatness. But as Southerners they are caught up in quite another historical experience: failure, defeat, and humiliation. Mark Twain summarized the impact of the Civil War in this way: "In the South the war is what A.D. is elsewhere; they date from it." Southerners have known condemnation; their heroes have been denounced as traitors; for many years they have been subjected to enforced idealization. For half of their experience since the Declaration of Independence, says Woodward, Southerners "lived intimately with a great social evil and the other half with its aftermath." The agony of all this is summarized by Woodward in his selection of a reminiscence by Arnold Toynbee:

I remember watching the Diamond Jubilee procession myself as a small boy. I remember the atmosphere. It was: well, here we are on top of the world, and we have arrived at this peak to stay there— forever! There is, of course, a thing called history, but history is something unpleasant that happens to other people. We are comfortably outside all that. I am sure, if I had been a small boy in New York in 1897 I should have felt the same. Of course, if I had been a small boy in the Southern part of the United States, I should not have felt the same; I should then have known from my parents that history had happened to my people in my part of the world.[35]

History indeed caught up with the South, as in the cyclic pattern it must with every people. But its visitation upon the South was bittersweet, for it left behind some images that may be savored, and these have stood the test of time.

Sometimes people ask "How long does history last to a nation? How long does preoccupation with a past endure?" The answer is history lasts as long as there are heroes to glory in, words to reverberate, ideals to inspire, and historians to recall all of it. Imagine a young man reading the wonderful prose of W. J. Cash:

Local patriotism was far from being dead in them, but nobody remembered now that they had ever gone out to die merely for Virginia or Carolina or Georgia. In their years together, a hundred control phrases, struck from the eloquent lips of their captains in the smoke and heat of battle, had burned themselves into their brains—phrases which would ever after be to them as the sounding of trumpets and the rolling of drums, to set their blood to mounting, their muscles to tensing, their eyes to stinging, to call forth in them the highest loyalties and the most active responses. And of these phrases the great master key was in every case the adjective Southern.[36]

He could not fail to feel a pride in his tradition. Or suppose he hears the story of a great-grandfather who rode with General Jeb Stuart's cavalry in its remarkable feat of galloping clear around a

Union army in northern Virginia. Or reads about the valiant people of Vicksburg who survived on mule meat as Ulysses Grant hammered that Mississippi city for six weeks. Or sees a columned plantation house that continues to haunt the present with images of a more chivalric day. Or visits a silent battlefield where the Confederacy was finally crushed under the weight of wave after wave of young Union bodies. To this day more than a hundred years later the collected imagery reaches into the minds of millions of Southerners and claims them as latter-day Confederates in pride and loyalty. A vanished South continues to shape a people's mind, giving continued testimony to the truth expressed by another Faulkner persona: "the past is never dead, it's not even past."

Many who explore the present American scene have a facile way of "writing off" the small town and its style of looking at things as if these did not matter any more. Such commentators are invariably urban in orientation and write from that perspective. As members of a city mass they tend to see individualism as a matter of "rights" rather than of personal distinctiveness. As students of the literature of change they define the world according to present consciousness. As rationalists they fail to appreciate the continuing gravitation of many to a way of life which, if it lacks logic, retains concrete substance. As intellectual sophisticates they assume a national homogenizing to the terms of certain well-advertised, fundamentally urban ideals. Generally, these components of the urban perspective have had the effect of closing off one's view of the continuing power of the small-town synthesis in modern America. This synthesis has been far too strong, too emotionally valid, and too humanly attractive to have succumbed to the urban advance, or to the urban malaise.

# CHAPTER FOUR

## STABLE MENTALITIES

### THE IDEA OF MENTAL RETREATS

The grass-roots American is thoroughly immersed in the concrete life, drawing sustenance from simple routine, simple friendliness, and simple pleasures, following, in his conventionality, the principle of conservation of energy. He does not seek new ideas and is usually uncomfortable with abstractions that do not readily relate back to the concrete world. Yet, paradoxically, ideas are singularly important in his life, once they have worked their way into the texture of his mind. When thoroughly understood, a set of ideas becomes the controlling influence for determination of his particular attitudes and views. Indeed, it is not too much to say that he does not possess ideas but is possessed by them. The influence of ideas is nowhere better expressed than by Henrik Ibsen, as he has one of his characters in *Ghosts* say

> But I almost think we are all of us ghosts. . . . It is not only what we have inherited from our father and mother that "walks" in us. It is all sorts of dead ideas, and lifeless old beliefs, and so forth. They have no vitality, but they cling to us all the same, and we

cannot shake them off. Whenever I take up a newspaper, I seem to see ghosts gliding between the lines. There must be ghosts all the country over, as thick as the sands of the sea. And then we are, one and all, so pitifully afraid of the light.[1]

The pages to follow will be concerned with "ghosts" that cling to grass-roots Americans, ghosts of ideas emerging from the several worlds that one may inhabit. But it is far too much to say that the ideas are lifeless or lack vitality, or do not have a high degree of pertinence to the real world. In fact many of the ideas to be discussed are more emotionally vibrant than the contemporary conceptions that would replace them.

Earlier, attention was given to the fixities of popular culture and of small-town culture. Both have left a strong imprint on American minds at the grass-roots level. But to complete the story a further net must be cast across the culture to capture several broad and quite diverse influences of compelling strength. These influences not only provide basic mental sets, but also in many cases reinforce some of the perspectives described in earlier chapters.

What will be explored here are patterns of thought and action flowing out of occupational, social, and religious loyalties. There is a set of ideas and attitudes that characterizes the small businessman, for example; there is a military mentality; there is a perspective that religious dogma commonly inspires. Each of these areas provides idea patterns that are fairly well-established and resistant to change, bringing a certain stability to the mental worlds of those whose loyalty has been attracted. In an important sense these mentalities may be called "retreats," in that they are well-fortified and secure fortresses of ideas and conceptions by which the chaos and contradictions of the world are made intelligible. Though it is far afield from the current inquiry, an illustration of how such retreats serve a person is afforded by an incident that occurred at the Versailles Peace Conference in 1919. The intensely nationalistic French leader Georges Clemenceau was being pressured by Woodrow Wilson to accept the League of Nations proposal so hopefully put forward by the American President. Clemenceau later recounted his confrontation with Wilson as follows:

I said to him, "Mr. Wilson, have you ever seen an elephant cross a swinging bamboo bridge?" Mr. Wilson said he had not. "Well, I'll tell you how he goes about it. First, he trots down into the stream to see if the foundations are all right; then he comes back and puts one foot on the bridge. If the result is reassuring, he ventures its mate. Then he gives the bridge a sharp jolt. If it stands that, he gives it his trust and advances. Now that's my idea about your bridge leading to the New Jerusalem. I may be, as they say I am, a springing tiger where my personal fortunes are concerned, but where the safety of France is at stake—Well, there never was an elephant more careful or cautious than I am going to be." [2]

Clemenceau's retreat was that of nationalism, and it shaped or colored nearly everything he did.

In this same way the retreats to be explored here provide a more or less continuing frame of reference according to which an individual views his world. From an intellectual standpoint the retreat is a theory about the way to get along or the way to perceive that corner of reality in which one lives. Once possessed, it provides a mental structure by which daily experience is interpreted and opposing ideas are set aside. Moreover, this structure grows stronger through its effectiveness in enabling the person to "make sense" of whatever he sees, hears, reads, and feels. From an outsider's standpoint, a given retreat might be regarded as extremely narrow, or as irrelevant to the real world, or as hampering social justice, and the outsider might then pronounce summary judgment that it is "escapist." Such a charge usually reflects an insensitivity to the necessities and mysteries of human consciousness. This point is elliptically but clearly made by the question that Jacques Barzun insists be answered by those who charge "escapism": "Suppose a primitive man, caught in a rainstorm, . . . has for the first time the idea of taking shelter in a cave: is he facing reality or escaping it?" [3]

That the outsider views the retreat as escapist or as inadequate does not greatly matter to the individual for whom that particular mentality has become operative, because for him it is a way in which his world is made knowable and manageable. It may not accord fully with scientific truths, and he may not be able to respond effectively to attacks upon it, but it retains its attractiveness, because, like any fairly closed system it has the merit of being comfortable to live with. Moreover, somewhere along the line acceptance of this retreat did involve deliberation, at least in the fundamental way that American essayist Ambrose Bierce described it: "The act of examining one's bread to determine which side it is buttered on." It may not manifest certain elegant ideals recommended by avant-garde thinkers, but the habitant of the retreat is not concerned. Americans at the grass-roots level have never been more than part-time idealists and are far too pragmatic not to be leery of sailing to "some false impossible shore." Finally, however much the fixed fortresses of beliefs and attitudes may be attacked by dedicated rationalists (as they regularly are), surrender is rare, for most of them have as part of their content something that may be called a "philosophy of defeat." Losing is not to be expected, but it has happened often enough that it has lost its corrosive power.

In his search for identity, any individual is exposed to many social organizations that promise, in exchange for his loyalty, a personal fulfillment and perhaps a potential self-aggrandizement that satisfy every identity demand. In a sense, social organizations—family, church, school, occupation, community, club, country, and others—battle for the individual's loyalty, though without much noticeable enmity. Most individuals eventually make a choice, tentatively at the beginning and then with commitment. Rarely do they choose only one organization, becoming, instead, actively conscious of the thinking, and of the necessities, of two or perhaps three such social entities. These become the "small, hard pieces" out of which emerge important controlling principles of life. In the twentieth century, granted its impersonal ways, individual loyalty has, in the opinion of historian Robert Wiebe, drifted away from attachment to local community, and attached to occupation as a source of truth.[4] Occupation has become the major "small, hard piece" around which Americans have built their lives in the twentieth century. While the present essay suggests a somewhat wider view, there is evident validity in the thesis that Americans listen more clearly than before to occupationally inspired truths, even to the extent that, as sociologist Robert Merton put it, "personal aspirations, interests, and sentiments are largely organized and stamped with the mark of . . . occupational outlook." [5] Obviously some occupations are of minimal importance in shaping one's perspective, but others make "total claims on their members and . . . attempt to encompass within their circle the whole personality." [6] Lying somewhere in between these two extremes are most of the occupations associated with the business world.

### The World of Business

It is not necessary to agree with Calvin Coolidge that "the business of America is business," nor with social critic Margaret Halsey that America has become a "one-institution society," in order to acknowledge the overwhelming importance of business in American life. If "business" is narrowly defined to include only managerial employees, secretaries, clerks, and other office people—the traditional white-collar jobs—then it refers to a bit more than twenty million individuals, or about one-fourth of the work force. If "business" is broadened to include those who are part of the entrepreneurial role of private enterprise, then more than half of the labor force is involved in it.[7] Whichever definition is preferred, the numbers of business-oriented people are impressive.

In how they see themselves American businessmen may be classified in three broad categories: the traditionalist; the small businessman; the modern manager.[8] Of these groups the traditionalist is much the smallest and its characteristic ideas will be given only brief consideration here. For the most part traditionalists operate manufacturing businesses of fewer than one thousand employees. As the term implies, the traditionalist finds the governmental economic manipulations of the past forty years very offensive, and believes that if the market system were left to its own natural processes, society would on the whole be better off. If such a free capitalistic system is not perfect, still it brings reasonably equitable distribution of the goods that the economy produces. Even with its defects, says the traditionalist, the system is better than a governmentally managed one, which, in its frenzies of economic leveling, gradually erodes the individual businessman's profit incentive. There is more, of course, to the traditionalist view, but it is not a large group, and since on most philosophical issues the traditionalist and the small businessman agree, it is appropriate to go on to the ideas of the latter.

While the voice of the small businessman is not clearly heard in the media debate on economic issues, still his number is not inconsiderable. He may be found in millions of street establishments, employing many more millions. Small businessmen operate more than 10,000 variety stores, 12,000 bakeries, 26,000 jewelry stores, 40,000 hardware stores, 50,000 furniture stores, 55,000 automobile dealerships, 110,000 clothing stores, and 150,000 gasoline service stations, not to mention hundreds of thousands of wholesalers of every kind, transportation firms, construction companies, real estate agencies, and the nearly half-million service companies of many kinds. In a well-advertised age of large corporations it remains a fact that of 3.2 million business establishments in the United States, 2.6 million, or 81 percent, may be called small by any definition, employing fewer than twenty persons per unit. Still another 15 percent of the total have fewer than one hundred employees, leaving 96 percent of business ownership in the hands of businesses that are thus modest in physical size.[9] In considering these statistics it must be understood that all of the small businesses combined have nowhere near the sales volume of less than 3 percent of the really big organizations. The point here, however, is not dollar volume, but rather the large numbers of citizens—including their employees, numbering upwards of 10 million people—who are tied in to a small-business frame of mind which exhibits strong strains of economic individualism. What follows does not, of course, speak for all small businessmen, but it reflects a point of view toward which many of them gravitate.

The fierce competitive battles the small businessman has fought in recent years against huge corporate entities and proliferating discount houses and supermarkets have deepened his already firm economic individualism. He has other enemies—big labor and big government—but in daily view is big business. As the conglomerates reach farther and farther into retail trade, the small businessman wonders why naked economic power should be allowed such dominance. He sees managerial hirelings of a distant corporation play a game of low price and no responsibility and wonders what has become of the principle of proprietorship. For his own part he participates actively in the life of his community, often belonging to a service organization such as Rotary, Kiwanis, or Lions. But he observes no such community sense emanating from the discount store with its acres of parking lot, nor does he find there clerks with personal warmth and willingness to help. Generally he sees very large and anonymous units as an immediate threat to himself, a long-range threat to traditional democracy, and which therefore ought to be broken up.

The small businessman's contact with big labor is often indirect, but he nonetheless sees it as an enemy. In recent years national labor unions have successfully promoted industry-wide contracts. The small businessman regards this development as pernicious in a number of ways. Local unions thus lose their autonomy in dealing with local conditions, and union members become faceless units in a national labor empire. The consumer loses because through the exercise of gigantic economic power the unions force wages for some skills unnaturally high, and prices must be raised to pay for the increased costs. And, of course, the small businessman himself loses, as the labor contract is negotiated by big management, which, through its volume operation, can more easily assimilate increased costs, thus placing the little man at a competitive disadvantage.

The litany of the small businessman's complaints has a major section devoted to the offenses of big government. It is not that Washington has been heedless of the little man; legislators know the political consequences of that. Especially noteworthy have been the fiscal assistance of the Small Business Administration and the trust-busting activities of the Attorney General's Office, though the latter's enforcement of the law has been highly variable with the political winds. But in the eyes of the local businessman all these efforts amount to using a bucket when a fire company is called for. Moreover, the government has taken far more than it has given the small businessman. It has taxed him heavily; it has encrusted normal business operations with layer upon layer of regulations, and at the same time created a bureaucratic system that snarls its patrons in paper work; it has upon occasion gone into business for itself, notably in the power production field; it has shown itself more concerned with the overseas interests of huge corporations than with the death struggles of local firms; most of all it has officiated at the wedding of big business and big labor, and because the marriage has been rocky from the start, has created a welfare system to carry it through its rough periods. A spokesman for the small businessman summarizes his basic perspective on these matters in these words: "Our loyalty is not a selfish loyalty to the little businessman—it is rather a loyalty to the America that he, and millions who preceded him, built. It is a loyalty to an America that big labor most of the time, big business part of the time, and big government all the time (whether consciously or not) are willing to sell down the river." [10]

The retreat wherein the small businessman is firmly settled is a contemporary expression of the agrarian spirit of America's early twentieth-century years.[11] This spirit placed great confidence in the individual, and with his resources of initiative, dedication, and willingness to work hard, a young man's future was in his own hands. In his own life the small businessman sees continuing confirmation of these values, and equally to the point, he sees the distresses produced by lack of them. The agrarian spirit also included a belief in the virtues of the domestic life and of moral training by parents. It trusted deeply in egalitarian democracy—in the little man being given a chance. It exalted the Constitution of the United States according to the letter; it glorified America as the land of the most and the best among nations and retained suspicions about the merit of international adventures that might compromise American values. It rejected the incipient collectivism of the early century, and as time went on, increasingly resented the lingering execution of Adam Smith by social and economic planners. It is offered by some in these later years of the century that the sentiments described are "out of date." The small businessmen, many of them, are not persuaded that basic individualism can ever be out of date.

However potent the small businessman remains as a political force, the numbers game has been won by the bureaucracies. While the term refers, in this case, to all those who are employed by large-scale organizations, still it is possible to distinguish between two major types—the organization man and what will be called here the "white-collar" worker. Organization men are all those who are a direct part of a hierarchal authority system in a modern bureaucracy. In essence, an individual in such a system *is* a bureaucrat, having a well-defined range of authority over specific subordinates and being answerable himself to some specific individual above him in the hierarchy. Authority originates at the top and is parceled out among the divisions that make up the whole, with each division in turn piecing out its segment of responsibility among its subdivisions. Titles vary, but a typical descending scale might run as follows: vice-president in charge of sales, division sales manager, regional sales manager, local sales manager. Each individual in a position below the vice-president is a "functionary" in the sense that he does not determine his goal, his responsibility being the means to be used to achieve organizationally established goals. More often than not these organization men tend to be well-educated—bachelor's or master's degree holders—for the reason that quite often their responsibilities require technical abilities or high literacy.

The organization man is locked into a demanding situation. In its competition with other firms in the market, his company must operate with certain "givens": it has an established product line; it has an established technology of production; it has an established budgetary projection; and, it has an established market structure. Changes may be made in these factors, but only at a considerable expense and over an extended period of time. In the meantime, as one observer put it, "the drive is for efficiency, and all operations are reduced to standard operating procedures that maximize profit." [12] The organization man is an important agent in the corporation's drive for efficiency, becoming the overseer of his subdivision's proper performance of its function. He is extremely alert to the perception of his effectiveness held by his superiors, especially his immediate superior. He also has long since developed a sense of loyalty to the organization, both because it has been benevolent (in pay and perquisites) and because it holds the promise of career success. Altogether it is not a situation that makes for dissent or for heightened individualism, as so many critics have noted.

The organization man has thus come to profess an ideology quite different from that of the small businessman. Though he does not appear to have abandoned allegiance to the virtues of initiative and thrift (and certainly not, hearing his rhetoric), he has in fact transferred their practice from the individual to the corporation as an entity, believing that thus his organization can rise to the top. As a subaltern in a big business system he understands and accepts large-scale government economic management, insofar as the organization is thus enabled to reach its corporate goals. As a member of a hierarchal system he has become deferential to authority, so much so that he has often surrendered his own idiosyncratic distinctiveness.[13] He is an accepted member of a miniature social system whose values of belongingness, togetherness, and scientism have narrowed his intellectual perspectives to the point where his judgments are singularly predictable. Accepting this new "social ethic," as spelled out by William H. Whyte, Jr., he has left his middle-class home "spiritually as well as physically, to take the vows of organization life. . . ." [14] Perhaps most demonstrative of the shift of many to an organization-mindedness is the change that has been observable in American self-help literature during this century. For the first third of the century the virtues described as crucial for success were hard work, determination, frugality, and the like— the so-called Protestant ethic. But these virtues have been obscured in the emphasis upon getting along with others. Now came a "Personality ethic" with prescriptions for being liked and sought after by management superiors, business associates, clients, and customers.[15] Symbolic of this change was Dale Carnegie's best-selling *How to Win Friends and Influence People* (1937), which in 1972 passed through its ninety-sixth printing.

However trackless it may seem at times there is a line in large corporate bureaucracies that separates the organization men from those that are in the organization but not of it. The latter are ordinarily the secretaries, the draftsmen, the clerks, the salespeople, the security guards, the office machine operators, the receptionists, the mechanical technicians, the laboratory assistants, the cashiers, etc., and sometimes the stagnated middle manager. These people are going nowhere in the organization and they know it. These are the people of whom sociologist C. Wright Mills spoke in his *White Collar* (1951). Their efforts, if efficient, will win them raises, but not real prestige, for the reason that they do not have their feet on the established ladder of major advancement. Historically, they "slipped quietly into modern society," the silent accompanists to big business crescendos of the early century. Their own pasts center around high school or business schools, and their future are indistinguishable from a thousand others in the organization. They are not an unhappy people, mildly frustrated perhaps with hierarchal foolishness, but for the most part settled in their daily work and reconciled to their basic situation.

The intellectual perspective of the white-collar worker is often narrow, but in a different way from that of the organization man. White-collar jobs are routine, and while calling for good sense, they afford little opportunity for initiative, for close reasoning, or for imaginative exercise. The white-collar worker achieves competence, but, outside of personal friendships at work, his interests lie elsewhere—in social life, in recreation, in particular hobbies, and in the small enjoyments that life can bring. Where his mind is not shaped by strong convictions from religion, from family, or from ethnic background, his views are likely to be powerfully influenced by the mass media—where else can his ideas come from? And so, on particular issues, he often reflects the worries and the conclusions of popular media forms. But in a broader pattern, the white-collar mind is shaped by those deeper themes of individualism, traditional virtue, and optimism, and all of the imagery relative thereto, that have been examined in an earlier chapter. Taken together these themes represent the most widespread retreat of an urban people.

What have been briefly considered here are three varieties of mentality, two of them anchored in certain occupational perceptions in the world of business and the third finding its chief ideas in a broader cultural setting. Where ego involvement is great, as in the case of the small businessman and the organization man, day-to-day usage of fixed reference points brings a mentality that is essentially occupational in character. Even more true is this when the occupation is also a way of life, as is the case with the military.

**The World of the Military—**
**The Military Mind**

There is a Rudyard Kipling poem about the British soldier that concludes with the following lines:

> "For it's Tommy this, an' Tommy that,
>     an' Chuck 'im out, the brute!
> But it's 'Savior of 'is country,' when
>     the guns begin to shoot." [16]

America's relations with its own military have followed a similarly ambiguous course. On the one hand, given the towering American pride in its ideals and strength, symbols of American might—massed naval, army, and air power—have been revered, and along with them the military man who makes it all work. And if the military man is further a symbol of excellent young American manhood, like the West Point cadet or Annapolis midshipman, so much the better, as Hollywood early discovered. Moreover, the American sense of mission has brought many overseas adventures during the past 130 years, and the firepower to implement these undertakings has been readily accepted. Nevertheless, the military have been put into kind of an antechamber to American life. Egalitarian sentiment is far too strong for wholehearted acceptance of a system that operates on a caste principle. The matter of "getting ahead" in making one's fortune is too much an American preoccupation for widespread acceptance of a military way of life. Finally, the moat of separation from other nations has often in the past bred a frugal isolationism that kept the military in straitened circumstances.

But World War II and the crises that followed it have made a difference. During the World War II period, more than 16.3 million Americans served in the armed forces; the Korean War saw 5.7 million in uniform; during the Vietnam conflict 8.8 million were in some branch of the service. As of 1973 there were 29 million living veterans of American military service, which works out to be 42.2 percent of American adult males. Further, the active military establishment in 1973 (excluding civilian employees) was 2.2 million.[17] How far influenced these millions of men have been by their military experience remains an open question. Certainly it is not as much as suggested in the catchword "Once a Marine, always a Marine." Yet underneath the overlays of occupational, social, and personal life there often remains in the former serviceman a residue of loyalty and pride, and of respect for the disciplinary traditions that are associated with military life. It is certain that military experience has more impact than credited by those who dismiss it out of hand as being painful in its entirety and of no long-term consequence. But however much military service has meant to present civilians, there is not any doubt that many of those now in active military service have their consciousness decisively shaped by the style of life that prevails on military posts. To one degree or another the military mind is possessed by all military men, inclining them to make over any other setting to conform to its patterns.

Military life is not simply an occupation—it is an existence with a character distinctively its own. It provides a relatively closed community, which has retained its distinctiveness despite major technological and demographic changes in the surrounding environment. Military personnel are far too mobile to be integrated into the civilian community alongside them. Though many service people live off base, they infrequently become property owners (given the fact that duty tours typically last three years) and thus lack a sense of a stake in the community. In important respects the local military take on the character of a foreign settlement; though they maintain business and educational relations with the larger community, still most of their needs can be and are taken care of through base facilities. Indeed, with commissaries, exchange department stores and service shops, recreational opportunities, church facilities, and medical services, it is almost possible that "a person or even a family can spend years there [on the military base] without ever leaving it and not suffer deprivation of basic needs!" [18] It is an advanced welfare system that continually binds one back to itself.

But the social distance between the military and the civilian is grounded in much more than physical factors. The ethos animating military life has a distinctive complexion: There is a formality about it, and a protocol, and a set of manners, which condition the relationships among its people. There is often a sense of personal fealty to the captain, the "old man," the corps, and, by a seemingly extravagant leap, to the person of the President of the United States. There is an intimation of being the standard-bearers of a strong and righteous nation. There is frequently a conviction that human beings should be viewed as they are, not as they are un-likely to become, and therefore, behind the peace table, the sword must be ever poised to strike. In sum there is a rectilinearity about military life that gives it a special quality, a point well-made in this reflection:

> . . . the soldier's life is more coherent than the civilian's and being more coherent is more tranquil. He is spared the agonies of in-decision which must torment the man who knows not what end his life serves. The military universe is, by all modern comparisons, a unified one; all of its parts conjoin. From the point of view of the individual there is certainty about it. There is something else too, something that modern society has been lamentably without: a sense of membership. No one is in doubt of what his role is, what his relation to others is, and in this respect there has been answered for the individual one of the most disruptive problems of modern society.[19]

The matter of membership and of its derivative—social solidar-ity—is an important feature of military life. Partly it is engendered by the idea consensus described above. But there are other influ-ences that further it. The disciplinary feature of service life is aimed at submerging individual inclinations to the priorities of group goals. To the extent that the submergence is successful there develops a powerful *esprit de corps,* which is a source of pride as well as a source of determination "not to let one's shipmates down." In the larger framework of the particular service as a whole (U.S. Coast Guard, Marines, Air Force, etc.) solidarity is furthered by strong friendships among academy comrades and com-pany members, by liberty hours spent in company in remote places, by service songs and mottoes, by pride in the uniform and the achievements it celebrates. It is a closeness that is fostered by an equivalency of goals and especially by idiom, jargon, and a way of using the language. Military men develop "a scheme of ex-pression . . . [which is] not teachable and cannot be learned in the same way as, for example, the vocabulary." Military language style is distinctive, and gradually one learns "to pray and curse in it and how to say things with every shade appropriate to the addressee and to the situation." [20] The sharing of the peculiar idiom is a subtle yet tangible element in military group unity. The sense of cooperative commitment is further solidified by the pageantry, the color and excitement of formal military ceremonies and parades, these a verisimilitude of glory unequaled in American life except by the inauguration of a President. The wives and the families, too, are affected by the pomp and circumstance, as military sociologist Morris Janowitz tells:

> Again and again, in data amassed from interviews and memoirs, one is struck by the extent to which women internalized the values of military honor and military ceremony. . . . The wife speaks with as much fervor as her husband when she says, "Fort Monroe was real Army, the honor guard marched frequently in the morning with the band. It was a grand sight to see the spick and span soldiers marching across the green of the parade grounds with the magnificent Chesapeake for a background." [21]

But it is not simply the ceremony that co-opts the wife: the military is also organized to assist the family. Aside from the commercial and recreational facilities already mentioned, there are offices to help with housing, furniture, travel, education, job placement, day care, and newcomer assistance. None of these services bear the stamp "For Officers Only." They are aimed at promoting overall loyalty. That they are successful is indicated by a survey of Army career enlisted men that showed a high percentage of them disposed "very favorably" toward service life.[22]

Military organization is a bureaucracy, and as such is separated into two groups, managers and subordinate workers, except that they are called officers and enlisted men. It is this caste system that provokes the most agitated commentaries by those in military life. Undoubtedly the criticism manifests an egalitarian resentment of privilege, but it also reflects an egalitarian resentment of taking any orders at all—"in many ways the animosity between lower-ranking enlisted men and NCO's (noncommissioned officers) has come to override the traditional enlisted hostility toward officers . . . it is an NCO rather than an officer who directly supervises an enlisted man on the job." [23]

A commissioned officer is a survivor of a medieval institution and as such has a special sanctity beyond his bureaucratic role. The delicateness of rank gradations provides further structuralization of relations (as between ensign, lieutenant [j.g.], lieutenant, etc.) beyond those imposed by one's position in the bureaucracy. The weaknesses of the system are tied in to the two roles: As a bureaucrat the commander may be inefficient in passing information (accompanying an order) downward through the channels of communication and as a result the man at the bottom receives a bald order, the rationale of which is unclear, and so he is resentful; nor can he expect a complaint or an observation to be efficiently transferred through the various levels to the top, and so he becomes, in his view, voiceless. As a commissioned officer, the commander has a charisma of rank, which, through condescension downwards and obsequiousness upwards, sometimes distorts honesty of communication with resultant inefficiency throughout the organization. Such potential defects notwithstanding, military organization produces "the most personalized control possible, as each commander knows the men *directly* under him and is responsible for everything within his command." [24] Under these circumstances of subletting power, even a corporal can be a terrible tyrant. But from a military standpoint, tyranny must be tolerated; unambiguous definition of responsibilities works—it gets the job done—and that, under a situation of foreign threat, is the important thing. Most military men—officers and enlisted alike—understand this and accept the system despite its inefficiencies.

It has been said earlier that military life has a rectilinear quality: it is squared off, relations are defined and made fully predictable. Nowhere is this more evident than in the protocol dictating social behavior. Service regulations and handbooks detail correct behavior for most situations, and tradition can be even more specific: a young ensign, unaccustomed to military nuances, one day "brought" a serious matter to the attention of his superior officer, whereupon he was admonished that a junior officer never "brings" a senior officer's attention to anything—he *"invites* his attention"* to a matter. In military courtesy handbooks a not inconsiderable number of directives are offered for smoothing the waters where official and private lives meet—at parties, receptions, informal meetings, and the like. The rules for a junior officer's courtesy calls on his commanding officer, for example, are well laid out, including such details as the allowable time period for calls, what kind of calling cards are acceptable, where they should be placed in the commanding officer's residence (in the silver tray on the hall table). For the most part the rules are followed, although flag officers do have some leeway. Another ensign, while based in Honolulu, received an invitation to an admiral's tea that began "You are invited and will attend . . ."—an unconscionable *diktat* by normal military standards. Of course, it did make a difference that the admiral had two highly marriageable daughters.

The tendency to use formulas that prescribe behavior extends to work and work relations as elsewhere. In considering this matter two points should be kept in mind: first, that a unit's effectiveness, and along with it, its *esprit de corps,* depends on efficiency of the division of labor; second, that military personnel are "here today and gone tomorrow"—transfers are constant. What these things mean is that if continuing efficiency is to be achieved, jobs must be routinized, broken down into specific steps, spelled out "by the numbers"—individualism can be very dangerous. And so, throughout the organization there are prescriptions. At the top it means that certain general rules are applied to specific situations. At the middle level it means that there are recipes for leadership as well as for department management. At the bottom level it means learning to follow fixed rules for nearly everything. (In early North African campaigns of World War II, inexperienced American soldiers went "by the numbers" to their own death against a skillful enemy who didn't follow the book rules for bayoneting.) Of course, nobody operates entirely by the rules; in fact, a commander who "lives by the book" is much feared and detested in the service. But the framework is always there, to be used as a general guide, and, if any inspection is forthcoming, to be observed with utmost care— at least within the perimeter of the "circle of compliance." *

* The "circle of compliance" is a common service term reflecting the inspectee's estimate of *exactly* what the inspector will inspect. Attention to anything else is omitted.

The exact patterning of tasks in the military brings some efficiency, but at least as much inefficiency. Anyone who is even mildly observant has learned that the road to advancement and/or preferred assignment is not paved by expropriating responsibility —one thus runs the risk of infringing upon the established (or arbitrarily assumed) prerogatives of someone higher up. And so one forms the "right" habits: before a request is approved it is processed through the proper channels; before a decision is made the commanding officer must set policy; before an action is taken detailed instructions must reach one's desk. A prudent enlisted man does no more than he is told. At its worst such a system leads to "Schweikism," after the fictional Czech soldier who fouled up the system by doing absolutely no more and no less than he was told. But characteristically, the system does achieve solid performance, even though it produces substantial under-usage of enlisted personnel and with that a lot of make-work to keep up appearances.

The concern of this discussion has been to examine the major dimensions of the military style of life with an eye to understanding the perspectives by which the military view of the world is shaped. The military man has been portrayed as something of an isolate from the American mainstream. He is a person who is steadfast in his Americanism and respectful of traditions; he is conscious of authority relations and responsive to authority as a principle; he is dubious concerning the inclinations of human nature and believes in careful control of them; he is deductive in mental functioning and places great value on predictability. And, for these reasons precisely, he represents a major variety of American stable mentalities.

### The World of Dogma

In America the battle began in the late nineteenth century. Christianity had long dominated American culture, and now in the 1880s and 1890s it was reinforced by the arrival of millions of southern and eastern European Catholics, who, though culturally and doctrinally distinct from their American Protestant brethren, nevertheless professed similar Christian values. Meanwhile the enemy was gathering, clustering in university halls and towers of the country, studying the treatises of Darwin, Comte, Freud, and Nietzsche. Soon began the drumfire against a complacent Christian civilization, first muffled as in a distant college classroom, then louder and closer as Theodore Dreiser, Van Wyck Brooks, Randolph Bourne, Sherwood Anderson, H. L. Mencken, and others of a young generation of intellectuals began their writing careers. Traditional Christianity came under sharp attack: the "higher criticism" claimed Old Testament inaccuracies; positivistic science rejected miracle accounts of the Nazarene's ministry; Freudian psychologists stripped veils from revivalist enthusiasms; and the Puritan stood accused of subverting all that was pure and creative in the American imagination. From a thousand scholarly and literary pens issued polemics that named Christianity as the archenemy of the arts and of the mind. From many more thousand scientific pens came facile explanations that dismissed God as a necessary Prime Mover.

The movement of the American academic mind against traditional religion has continued through the middle years of the twentieth century, though moderating its earlier abusiveness. In a democratic spirit of tolerance, direct attacks upon religion were abandoned; the intellectuals' criterion became that of rational humanism, with religion becoming an indirect bogieman for its failure to be either sufficiently "rational" or sufficiently "humanistic" according to contemporary definitions. In this value structure religion was seen as "archaic" or "irrelevant," and the image given off by intellectuals was one of calculated indifference toward religion rather than hostility. Still, the old animus remained, as reflected in the recent remarks of a famed social psychologist who censured the churchgoer for having "a self-centered preoccupation with saving his own soul, and an alienated, other-worldly orientation coupled with indifference toward—a tacit endorsement of—a social system that would perpetuate social inequality and injustice." [25] What ruffles many intellectuals about religion is that the believer has an ideologically fixed, long-term perspective, something that seems somehow unreasonable to large numbers of modern social scientists.[26]

The long-sustained put-down of religion by intellectuals has been a major factor in its decline in the twentieth century. By external standards—membership and attendance—churches held on very well through the 1950s, but in 1970 had shown evident decline by both of these criteria. A declining percentage of Americans belonged to a church, and of these church members far fewer than half participated in weekly services.[27] Moreover, even in the apparently good years of the 1940s and 1950s Protestant mainstream churches were preaching a dogma that had undergone notable secularization. During the 1920s liberal theorists had captured control of major Protestant seminaries, replacing doctrinal specifics with humanistic concerns. Theologian H. Richard Niebuhr described the Protestantism that emerged in this way: "A God without wrath [brings] men without sin into a kingdom without judgment through the ministrations of a Christ without a cross." Softening of Christianity's traditional rigor was also manifested by the rise, in the late 1940s, of a popular media Protestantism, as preached by Norman Vincent Peale and others, which emphasized a feeling of well-being as the central goal of religion.[28] Thus, for many, religion had become a sociological institution whose ministrations had more to do with peace of mind than with commandments for living.

Yet in the face of this three-quarter century withdrawal from piety there have remained large numbers of religious believers whose lives are bounded on every side by the absolutes of dogma. There is no gainsaying the fervor of millions of Protestant fundamentalists, nor of Mormons, nor of traditional Roman Catholics. Each of these religions provides a major retreat for many millions of Americans. The main ideas of each of these religions will be discussed in the paragraphs to follow, beginning with Catholicism, which is the largest firmly dogmatic religion in America. Before summarizing mainstream Catholic views, however, a moment must be taken to review the church's turmoil in America during the past fifteen years.

Vatican II, convened in the early 1960s, was called for the express purpose of "updating" the church to the ways of life of the modern world. It was an essentially conservative proceeding, which, while recasting the fundamentals of dogma into contemporary language, also worked out a program for liturgical modifications and sought closer relations with other religious faiths. Generally, the public posture of the church was to be that of openness, both in regard to activity of participants in the worship services and to people of other theological persuasions. Reactions to both forms of openness were frequently negative, and though the storms abated, church attendance suffered a decline because of them. What had a much more damaging effect was a secularist-inspired flirtation with heresy. During and after the Council, Catholic intellectuals, both inside and outside the clergy, failing to understand that openness was not to be applied to dogma, began to preach, teach, and write views sharply different from and even opposed to the orthodox doctrine.[29] At the same time they began to promote a sociological Catholicism, with overtones of political liberalism, which many found impertinent both from the standpoint of politics and from the standpoint of development of filial piety. Then, in 1968, the reiteration by Pope Paul VI of the church's traditional strong stance against artificial contraception had further impact, at least according to the research of sociologist Andrew Greeley.[30] By 1973 average weekly Mass participation had declined to 48 percent of the 48.5 million Catholics in the United States.[31] But the shake-out of marginal Catholics is seemingly over, and it is very probable that most of the 24 million or so who still use the pews on Sunday are hard-core believers for whom dogma is crucial.

There are few religions, or ways of life, as structured as traditional Catholicism or as shaped by absolutist principles. While granting the possibility, rather the necessity, of achieving holiness, the church stresses man's propensity to evil. In fact, says the church, evil resides first in the human soul, and only secondarily in society, and only in society because of many individuals' failure to follow the rule of Christ. It is not that social reform may not be sought; it is a matter of where it should begin: "Lord, reform the world, beginning with me." Appetites of man's physical and intellectual natures are not in themselves evil but are to be subordinated to the necessities of his moral nature. Inherently weak in the roots of his being, man cannot succeed without God's assistance, this assistance (grace) being made available through the avenue of the sacraments, which themselves are precisely defined. Because of the riches of Christ's sacrifice, great possibilities have been opened to the individual—here is the feature that gives Catholicism its cosmic optimism. But redemption is always a personal task, and faith, while crucial, must be accompanied by strong salvatory works. Acceptance of a body of specific truths is absolutely requisite for the Catholic, these truths relating mainly to the relation of Christ to mankind and the validity of the church as Christ's agent. There is more, of course, but the foregoing is sufficient to give an idea of the highly structured nature of Catholicism and of the point of view that follows from these specifics.

There are a number of derivatory attitudes that most often accompany basic Catholic thought. Quite evidently, a faith that emphasizes absolutist truths and values is not going to be the most comfortable home for a modern intellectual, nor does he readily suffer the stricture of obedience to hierarchal authority. The rank-and-file Catholic is distressed when the intellectual by his ceaseless questioning appears to subvert highly valued beliefs. Thus, "a wealth of evidence [suggests] a strong anti-intellectual strain" among the Catholic population.[32] Further, because the things of the world and the flesh often war against the spirit, the Catholic is more readily disposed to censorship and to sumptuary legislation. Still further, since evil is in its origins a matter of individual will, social problems are apt to be viewed by many Catholics in the context of moral weakness rather than societal failure. Thus, in the view of political scientist Michael Parenti, "the Catholic tradition in American could hardly be characterized as liberal reformist. . . ."[33]

Recognizing this highly contained Catholic conceptualization of the world, a number of observers have identified Catholicism with a strong traditionalist theme in American history. The French Dominican R. L. Bruckberger had "the impression that American Catholics are more Puritan than anybody else and that they are very close to setting themselves up as the champions of Puritanism."[34] Sociologist Seymour Martin Lipset described them as having "taken on the coloration of a fundamentalist orthodox religion comparable in tone and style, if not in theology, to the nineteenth-century evangelical Protestant sects."[35] More recently, Parenti found "striking resemblances in underlying belief orientation between fundamentalist * Protestantism and Catholicism." [36] Obviously, there are differences between the two, as in the matters of hierarchal control, the role of the ministry, the degree or emphasis upon liturgy, and specifics of dogma. However, certain major themes are the same, among them the understanding of inherent human tendencies to evil, doctrine as fixed and final, the Bible as the inspired word of God, suspicion of intellectualist speculations, and personal responsibility for salvation. It is not surprising that many Catholics feel much more comfortable with fundamentalists than with some of the recent sociologically-oriented products of Roman Catholic seminaries.

American Protestant fundamentalism as a self-conscious group is a creation of the twentieth century, but its real origins are farther back. In the late nineteenth century urban Protestantism, deeply shaken by naturalistic thought, began to place as much confidence in scientific revelation as in biblical revelation. Rural Protestants, however, stood fast in the faith of their fathers. After some preliminary skirmishing at the turn of the century, the issue was joined in 1909 when two Californians, Lyman and Mills Stewart, sponsored a series of books and papers, which, in attacking modernist views, fell back on a set of propositions that were seen as the uncompromisable "fundamentals" of the Christian religion. Hence the name. The contest between the modernist and fundamentalist factions in Protestant denominations continued through the 1920s, but by the end of the decade the modernists were everywhere triumphant, or nearly so. Defeated in the battle for administrative control of the denominations, fundamentalists separated from the main bodies and formed their own organizations, establishing seminaries and separate congregations and periodicals—in general, entirely distinct structures. They were a determined people, and despite the fact that twentieth-century rationalism has denigrated them as rustic and unintelligent, they have emerged from their setback with a vigor and an *élan* that

---

* The term "fundamentalist" is used here for the sake of consistency, but "conservative" would serve as well. Some Protestants prefer the latter, as they believe "fundamentalist" has an overtone of political evangelism. Still others use the term "evangelical" to describe conservative-minded Protestants.

far exceeds that of their adversaries. As of the mid-1960s their numbers ranged somewhere between 20 million and 30 million people, depending on who is included as a fundamentalist.[37] In all likelihood they exceed their liberal brethren in numbers, and certainly in intensity.

Though there is variation among the several denominations on doctrinal matters, the principles of fundamentalism include the following: the inerrancy of the Bible as the inspired word of God; the deity of Jesus Christ born of the Virgin Mary; the redemptory character of Christ's crucifixion, which was a substitutionary atonement for the sins of the individual; the resurrection of Christ followed by His ascension to the judgment seat of mankind; the second coming of Christ. Great emphasis is placed upon the "conversion" experience, which is expected to bring a deep-seated change of heart in a believer. Many fundamentalists place great confidence in a charismatic leader, of the Billy Graham type, but far more of them look to the pastors of their congregations for inspiration and leadership.

Fundamentalism stresses religion as a total life experience: activities that, in the fundamentalist view, imperil spiritual life, such as drinking and gambling, are to be avoided; dress and manner should not ostentatiously celebrate the attractions of man's physical nature; each person should consider himself as a Christian witness and something of a personal evangelist; the faithful should in some respects remain aloof from the surrounding pagan society; tithing is expected, even required. Preoccupation with the anatomy of personal spiritual development precludes extensive concern with social reform, though fundamentalists are not opposed to it *per se*. Given their concern with the weaknesses of human nature, they may be expected to endorse the "work ethic," and they do. Very generally, the fundamentalist is a dedicated, community-motivated, spiritually assured individual who approaches reality with a well-articulated frame of reference that works for him. He is not likely to suffer the agonies of the indecisive.

Religious belief may be understood as significant at any one of four levels. At the first level it is "stimulus-response verbalism," this being the typical level of childhood and some adults; a second level of belief is "intellectual comprehension," at which stage the individual understands the relations of the themes and propositions which compose the religion; the third level is that of "behavioral demonstration," wherein the believer acts in accordance with the specific rules of the faith; the fourth and final level is that of "comprehensive integration," meaning that the beliefs have become so thoroughly internalized that the individual has "put on the new man" of biblical allusion, his life and his religion woven together closely, along the lines of a retreat in which one constantly lives.[38] With religion looked at in this way there are a number of other churches that should be included whenever one is discussing "comprehensive integration." Two to three million Orthodox Jews, along with many others described as "Conservative," live lives firmly grounded in dogmatic precept. So too do the Witnesses of Jehovah, but they are small in number—about 500,000 members. Other "new fundamentalist" groups, such as the "Jesus People," might be included, but they too are small. Not small are the Churches of Jesus Christ of Latter-Day Saints, who now number 3.5 million and who continue to grow.

The Mormon understanding of Christ's relations with mankind is different from that of the other Christian religions. They see Christ as having ministered to the people of the New World following his resurrection. The Book of Mormon, found by Joseph Smith in 1827, adds to what Christians already know through their own Bible. Mormons accept the ideas of the Trinity, Christ's atonement for sin, His resurrection, and the importance of strenuous individual effort to achieve salvation (though their theory does not include acceptance of original sin). For all its decisive difference in dogma, the Mormon Church has several similarities to the Catholic Church. Both have highly detailed doctrines, an authoritative hierarchy, and officially prescribed rites. Both condemn divorce, take special note of holy days, and make elaborate provision for education of the young. Both teach their faithful to wonder about the validity of this world's values, as do the Protestant fundamentalists.

Mormonism is a comprehensive doctrine, one with an abundance of absolutes. It reaches into every corner of the believer's life. A Mormon is expected to be an activist, achieving his salvation through the "work, health, recreation, and education complex."

He must avoid whatever might harm his body, including tobacco, alcohol, coffee, tea, and other hot beverages. Cereal and grain foods are to be used in preference to meats. Intellectual advancement in this world brings a higher place in the world to come, so education is given very high emphasis and continues throughout life. Church participation is intense: Sunday church service is lengthy and participatory; tithing is required at a 10 percent level for the general fund, along with another 2 percent to the local chapel; a two-year missionary term is served by many of the younger Mormons. Group activities are so much encouraged that Mormons have something of a communitarian tinge, which in fact some of its smaller communities tried in the nineteenth century. But emphasis upon community should not hide the fact that Mormonism has an intensely individualistic strain, an outgrowth perhaps of the stress on individual progress on this earth being reflected in the afterlife. Mormons place a high value on work and self-sufficiency. They strongly support capitalism, and there is major opposition to legislation that enforces collectivism, such as the closed shop. Generally, the Mormon Church is a quite accurate manifestation of an adage in which it takes pride: "In necessary things, unity; in other things, liberty; in all things, charity." [39]

These three large religions—Catholicism, fundamentalist Protestantism, and Mormonism—have served as strong stabilizing agents in American life. Along with other smaller religions having highly structured belief systems, they provide their faithful with a frame of reference that surpasses the here-and-now in favor of values they see as eternal. They remain forceful enemies of relativistic thought, sustaining a sense of absolutes among a people often preoccupied with change.

### Other Worlds

The aim of the present chapter has been to examine the retreats—of absolutes and of strong assurance—that individuals have built through their association with the world of business, with military life, and with religious dogma. Besides these there are other worlds in which people reside, each of them having major shaping influence on American minds. Among the most important of them are the world of Americanism and the world of the ethnic.

## Americanism

When the subject of twentieth-century Americanism is raised, the predicate that follows must include the name of the American Legion. The Legion has been tremendously effective at the grass-roots level in preaching Americanism over the past half century. Partly its influence lies in its membership of more than five million veterans, who find in the Legion a reservoir of memories of younger days, days of idealism, camaraderie, and shared hardship, all of these representing an experience that marked the rites of passage from adolescence into manhood. Legionnaires feel a nostalgia for those days of youth: though the military experience may have been difficult, from the sacrifice it called forth comes in later years a feeling of pride in having been part of a great and testing enterprise, and a feeling of having paid one's dues for the blessings this country confers. If the military posture and manner have vanished, a residue of the experience remains, this in the form of loyalty to the goals and themes for which the Legion stands.

Legionnaire loyalty is important, but of far greater importance are the widespread political, social, and educational efforts of the American Legion since its inception in 1919. Its political impact in support of what it sees as American values has been and continues to be powerful. It successfully backed the national origins quota legislation of 1923, and for those few who now could immigrate it sponsored citizenship and naturalization classes. It helped create the Veterans Bureau, the predecessor to the present Veterans Administration. Its campaign against communists and associated left-wingers in the 1930s was effective enough that the Legion became a prime target of Marxist intellectuals of that time, one of whom in a book-length diatribe denounced it as "Fascist and unpatriotic." [40] Throughout the thirties the Legion fought, though unsuccessfully, for national preparedness. Later, when the ensuing war was nearing its conclusion, it conceived and sponsored the G. I.

Bill of Rights, which since becoming law in 1944, has provided benefits for eleven million veterans. The Legion was a strong promoter of universal military training and a moving force behind the enactment of a strong Reserve Forces Act of 1955. Finally, the Legion was a major voice in insisting that America live up to her military commitments to overseas nations, including South Vietnam. Generally, then, the American Legion has been a forceful advocate of a strong military posture.

The Legion has been equally active in social and educational programs that foster what it early called "Americanism." Within a few months after its formation after World War I it resolved to establish a "National Americanism Commission" charged with the tasks of combating "all anti-American tendencies," instilling "ideals of Americanism in the citizen population," and promoting "the teaching of Americanism in all schools." In implementation of these purposes the Commission promoted a seemingly endless list of activities, almost all of them remarkably successful: creation of a junior legion baseball system; promotion of flag days, along with celebrations organized for Armistice Day, Memorial Day, and Columbus Day; fireworks festivals on July Fourth; Christmas tag collections; community betterment programs; assistance to Boy Scouts, Girl Scouts, and 4-H Clubs; creation of "Boys' States" and "Girls' States" days all over the country; sponsorship of a national oratorical contest, of Legion School Medal Awards, and of essay contests; finally, the Legion fought for "reasonably favorable presentation of American history" in the schools—successfully one hastens to say—but in the process taking much abuse from increasingly rootless twentieth-century intellectuals.[41] The list of activities above is only partial. It is not at all surprising that the Legion has become a household word in American life, and one with a very favorable connotation.

The importance of the Legion's efforts is evident when one recognizes the overwhelming dedication there is to Americanism in the United States. It is not simply a patriotism, but more, something that a number of observers have called the "civil religion" of America. This term was coined by sociologist Robert Bellah in a 1967 essay.[42] Since then the idea has been carefully examined for its meaning and its content, and though agreement is imperfect, most observers view America en masse as professing a secular faith that has many of the trappings of religion. Though the major religions may have contributed something to its ethos, and continue to reinforce its values, still this "civil religion" is distinct from them, though not antagonistic. The civil religion has various names —the American Way of Life, Americanism, the American Credo, or simply the American Religion. The common premise of any of these terms is that there is something unique, and, in a way, sublime, about the whole matter of being American.

The millions who fall back into the ramparts of this American civil religion are well-fortified. Perhaps the keystone of the belief system is trust in political democracy. This idea has many, many meanings, among the most important of them being the wide extension of the voting franchise and confidence in the political judgment of grass-roots America. Closely intertwined with the principle of democracy is the ideal of a social egalitarianism that endorses classlessness and a commonality of manner, as if to forbid any putting on of airs. A further article of the American faith is belief in individualism, a mainstream theme, yet one which in a peculiar way divides Americans into two opposing factions, though they remain of the same church. One group emphasizes the self-reliance dimension of individualism, insisting that government be a minimal factor in the competitive contest; the other group stresses the anti-authoritarian (or nonconformist) aspect of individualism, thus being preoccupied with protection of rights of speech, privacy, and choice against the incursions of government and of other cultural institutions. Both groups claim the Constitution as their primary source of protection, and of veneration too.[43]

The elements cited—democracy, egalitarianism, individualism —are dogma, a part of the grass-roots American's creed. But there are other doctrinal components, and if acceptance of them is not universal, it is certainly widespread. A majority, while accepting a vague principle of equal access to the good things of life, is fervently committed to the more immediate principle that work and money are inseparably intertwined; thus, "free rides," whether in the form of food stamps, or welfare money, or other, are suspect. Tolerance of religious difference, and, somewhat more recently, of ethnic difference, is another grass-roots staple, though many regard this profession as being of the lips rather than of the heart. A further tenet is a derivative of American optimism and involves an assumption that whatever evil appears can be erased, and all the significant human problems solved (not merely managed), if only the right legislative chord can be struck. All of these core and common beliefs combine to form a strong mental structure that defines Americans' expectations of what life should hold for them, a point well-made by Will Herberg: "The American Way of Life . . . synthesizes all that commends itself to the American as the right, the good, and the true in actual life. It embraces such seemingly incongruous elements as sanitary plumbing and freedom of opportunity, Coca-Cola and an intense faith in education—all felt as moral questions relating to the proper way of life." [44]

Just as is true of all religions, there are variations of emphasis on doctrinal specifics, and especially are there gradations in intensity of belief. But for all believers there is an extensive symbolization of the inner truths of the faith. The American flag symbolizes both unity and sacrifice; patriotic songs serve as hymns, one of them that summons the people to battle even called a "hymn"; national heroes are venerated as saints; national holidays are feast days for remembrance of past greatness. All of this is not simply a matter of patriotism; there is much more to it, as has been pointed out by several historians. Americanism has a mystical assumption of "chosenness": here is a people set apart by God, designated by Him to fulfill Divine ideas and goals. This conception of America as "God's New Israel" has been elaborately traced from a Puritan minister's 1669 declaration that "God sifted a whole nation that he might send choice grain into this wilderness," through Abraham Lincoln's Gettysburg Address and Woodrow Wilson's ringing announcement that America "must make the world safe for democracy," to more recent presidential calls for "crusades" here and overseas.[45] This American sense of mission, with the righteousness it generates, lends powerful energies to achievement of American ideals both at home and abroad, causing one Englishman to remark that Americans "have a sort of permanent intoxication, a sort of invisible champagne. . . . Americans do not need to drink to inspire them to do anything." Their inspirations have brought on many foreign adventures. Yet it must also be remembered that there is a side to "chosenness" that bids one to stand aloof from lesser peoples, leading to a lively isolationism expressed by Will Rogers in the 1930s with this counsel to President Roosevelt: "Mr. Franklin D, shut your front door to all foreign ambassadors running to you with news. Just send 'em these words: 'Boys, it's your cats that's fighting. You pull 'em apart.' "

The ideas that form the substance of Americanism are not simply catchwords of warmed-over annual holiday verbalisms, but represent a deep and enduring idea system in grass-roots America. They compose the elements of a legitimate American idealism, which, if not of day-to-day influence, becomes powerfully operative on occasions when national pride is affronted or when national conscience is decisively reached. It is an idealism that has had immense appeal to immigrants and has brought easy acceptance on their part of their adopted country. The theme of the next section is that of ethnic distinctiveness, but exploration of this theme should not obscure the abiding faith of the ethnic in American ideals.

## The World of the Ethnic

A persistent theme in cultural commentary in recent years is the continued and even resurgent strength of ethnic groups in the United States. Influenced or perhaps provoked by the rise of black consciousness and of growing black visibility in urban centers, the ethnics have become increasingly self-conscious and increasingly militant. The 1970 census showed slightly more than 16 percent of American population to be of "foreign stock" (this includes the foreign born and the native population born of foreign or mixed parentage).[46] More than this, a 1971 Census Bureau survey reported that 60 percent of the population identified themselves with a single ethnic origin—well over half of the total white population so representing themselves.[47] Geographically, the ethnics are most heavily concentrated in the urban Northeast (34 percent) and in the Great Lakes area. Most often the male family members are blue-collar workers, nearly half of the ethnics of Polish, Italian, and Irish origins being so employed.

The critical element in ethnicity is not, however, where one resides or what one does for a living; rather it is a question of how much investment of self there is in the ethnic line from which one comes. It can be negligible, as in the case cited by one observer of the Jew to whom Jewishness meant nothing more than a "midnight longing for a hot pastrami sandwich." Or it can be enormous, as reflected in sacrifices made by far-removed American Jews in behalf of a beleaguered Israel. That there is a growing consciousness of ethnicity is reflected in interest in genealogical searches, in foreign travel to the fatherland, in careful selection of folk culture names for children, and in the continued vitality of ethnic organizations.

The failure of the melting pot to dissolve these groups into homogeny is variously explained. However much acculturation in language and behavioral patterns is found necessary, the ethnic has often maintained strong local "substructures." These have included immediate family, extended family, neighborhood clubs, fraternal associations, churches, schools, old folks homes, taverns, and other social connectives. In the words of political scientist Michael Parenti, "From birth in the sectarian hospital to . . . sectarian cemetery—the ethnic, if he so desires, may live within the confines of his sub-society matrix—and many do." [48] This reflects what one observer has called the fundamental inclination in human life—"a desire to live privately . . . with one's family and friends." A further factor in ethnic separateness is that mainstream America never gave the immigrants a warmhearted welcome. Though colleges and, eventually, even country clubs and cotillions might be open to them, it was "unlikely that from childhood to adult one will have escaped a realization that some kind of stigma is attached to one's minority identity, that one is in some way 'marginal.' " [49] This traditionally brought renewed efforts to acceptance on the part of the ethnic, but in recent years he has been dubious about taking on a faceless but numbered "mass man" organization stereotype in exchange for the richness, the tradition, and the distinctive individuality of a folk culture.

One of the keynotes of ethnic style in America has been loyalty to what sociologist Andrew Greeley has called "social turf." [50] This means the local area some particular nationality calls its own, of course, but it encompasses much more. It includes the web of social relationships both formal and informal that sustain the life of the ethnic community: favored produce shops and bakeries, common meeting points and hangouts, public characters, standard jokes, common enemies, landmarks and boundaries, family doctors, architectural forms, favorite cops, neighborhood holidays, and perhaps a baseball team. An Irishman who grew up in Omaha recalled his youthful experience of competing in baseball against teams from the many ethnic sections of that Midwestern city: when one slid into second base he *always* came in with his spikes high and he *never* dug in at the plate. The "social turf" of childhood remains with a person forever, as pointed out by Nicholas Pileggi, describing young suburban Italians who each weekend return to the old home grounds, "not only for the bread, tiny bitter onions, bushels of snails, live eels and dried cod, but also to enjoy a weekend heritage that their education, bland wives, and the English language have begun to deny them. . . . it is only with a trunk filled with Italian market produce that a Saturday Italian can face six days in the suburbs." [51] The attachment spoken of here is very much the same as that described earlier in this book as a part of the small-town ethos. This parallel is a central theme of Herbert Gans in *The Urban Villagers* (of New York): "For most West Enders, then, life in the area resembled that found in the village or small town. . . ." Given this fond bondage to "social turf," it is not surprising that ethnics fiercely resist forced busing.

Because the point is so strongly emphasized among students of ethnic groups, one must dwell on the matter of the ethnic community sense. Commitment to family is intense, even where relationships between particular individuals have been or are volatile. Angry outbursts and bitter arguments do not destroy a relationship unless the individuals engaging in the fireworks are already atomized anyway. But ethnics are not atomized. Even where generational alienation is great, juveniles' allegiance to community is not compromised. Parenti found this generally so, marking it with a specific illustration: speaking of a Polish-American industrial town, he concludes: "The Polish children treat their immigrant parents with either patronization or contempt, speak American slang, are addicted to American popular music, and popular culture, accept fully the American way of piling up money and material goods when possible. Yet they keep almost all their social contacts within the confines of the Polish-American community and have no direct exposure to, and little interest in, middle-class American society." [52] This communitarian network, whether the connections be to family, relatives, or friends, represents the vital principle of ethnic life. It suggests an organic view of life very different from that of many in middle-class America. The contrast is searchingly described by Michael Novak:

> "People" is an organic, nongeometric, nonrational, nonmechanical concept. Historical peoples grow like hedges: concretely, contingently, thickly, in all directions, in ways that are entangled and dense and labyrinthine. A hedge cannot be taken apart like the engine of a Ford. A people carries with it prejudices, customs, habits, ways of perceiving and imagining and acting. . . .
>
> By contrast, a mass is a people whose organic, affective, habitual connections have been severed. A mass is an assemblage of discrete units. Their source of unity is given from outside, by those experts whose task is to rationalize and to manipulate social relationships. . . . Built into the language of Anglo-Saxon social work (Orwell encouraged us to scrutinize such language coldly) is a scheme of manipulation. Authority belongs to the rationalizers. The masses are expected to be grateful for plans contrived to make their lives more affluent and pleasant. The social system is a functional mechanism.
>
> Who are the parts, and who the mechanics? [53]

Among the most important of the "mechanics," concluded Novak elsewhere, are the intellectuals.

Most ethnic groups (one is tempted to say almost all) have a deep-seated distrust and fear of intellectuals. Partly this is because of the intellectuals' efforts to make over ethnics into certified pure Americans responsive to official liberal ideology; partly it is the intellectuals' mask of moral superiority while undertaking ruthless modernization of the ethnic psyche; partly it is because of the intellectuals' veneration of the young, whom the ethnics find lovable, but often banal in their enthusiasms and irresponsible in their behavior; partly it is because of the intellectuals' passion for the officially sanctioned "deprived" groups—the black, the Indian, and the Chicano—with whom the ethnic has many points of friction; partly it is because the intellectuals spend their days "toying" with ideas, while he, the ethnic, puts in eight hours of hard physical labor. Such are the complaints the intellectual would hear after a drink or two had eroded the ethnic veneer of civility. But it is not likely that the blue-collar ethnic would ever talk of that which makes unbridgeable the gulf between himself and the intellectual, as it calls for greater articulative powers than he is likely to possess. The American small townsman had the same problem and almost the same grievance. But a facile ethnic would put it this way: the intellectual has an exceedingly narrow and rationalistic ideology of human nature. He fails to understand—perhaps, because of his implicit positivism, is incapable of understanding—the mystery, the folly, the desperation, the intuitive wisdom, the transcendence, the unprovable uniqueness, of the human animal. He is insensitive to the intimacy of communion with one's own individuality-as-a-collectively-formed-reality. No one says this better than the Slovak-American Novak:

> Philosophers tend to speak of human action as a matter of principles or perhaps as a matter of emotional preferences. But besides the pragmatic effects of actions, there is also their intensity. Besides the principle in view, there is also the style of their execution. Besides the strategy, there is also the preferred, instinctive, comfortable ways of proceeding. Besides the tactics, there is the sense of timing, rhythm, and pace. Besides the circumstances there are the impulses and passions. Besides the rational, discursive content, there are the gestures, winks, impassivities. Besides the agent there is the network of others of which he is a part. Besides the calculus of interests, there are also different rules for, and ways of experiencing pleasures and pains. Besides happiness, or fruitful consequences, there are also the joys of doing things just for the hell of it.[54]

Essentially it is a matter of the ethnic viewing life organically, as being of a piece with layers of significant others. With this comes a veneration of custom, tradition, inwardness, and a corresponding distaste for rationalistic dissection of the organic reality that is life itself. How foreign, then, is the intellectuals' surgical separation of life into structures, roles, reference groups, and his corresponding glorification of the individual—in short, how foreign to the ethnic is an atomic theory of humanity that canonizes rationalistic individualism.

The ethnic, then, sees the world through different lenses than those prescribed on college campuses. Thus he is apt to view many matters in a different light: (1) he (and many shes) regards women's liberation as nonsense, a contrivance of upper-middle-class ennui and a perversion of true selfhood—it promises what it cannot (and should not) deliver and offends the principle of organicism; (2) too much is made of corruption in high places. The stench may be abominable, but it has always been that way and is the legitimate price people pay for government. The ethnic truly understood John Kennedy's appointment of his brother as Attorney General, for he (the ethnic) places family loyalty on a high plane too; (3) except when it agrees with his prejudices (which is rarely), the ethnic is suspicious of the news media, which is united in unholy wedlock with the intellectuals, and, covertly, offers the same moral preachments. All of the commentators and editors together do not have the impact and the savor of one brutal hit on a network football game; (4) his attachment to his own culture notwithstanding, the ethnic is intensely patriotic. He wears his Americanism on his sleeve and is resentful of those who deride basic national virtues. He does acknowledge, though, that the system has defects, not the least of which is a surfeit of freedom of revolutionary speech; (5) the ethnic believes in authority and is not squeamish about using it in his own home. He thinks something is wrong with people who think that sweetness and light and reason are the keys to rearing children. The young respond to authority and need it if they are to be decent adults. The ethnic thinks permissiveness is folly, as reflected in the statement of an officer of the Confederation of American Ethnic Groups: "They're 100 percent against permissiveness . . . Not 99 44/100 percent, but 100 percent. I know a lot of families who, if their kid came home with long hair, they'd chase him right out." [55] As with the family, so with society. If many parents have failed to discipline their children, then society must do it, and ruthlessly—in the schools, in the streets, in the courts. The ethnic knows that being tough is a rule of life.

The worlds described here, the worlds of business, of the military, of dogma, of Americanism, and of the ethnic, play a crucial role in defining the perspectives of grass-roots Americans. But there are still other worlds that provide fixed idea sets to those that inhabit them. The world of the housewife brings with it a set of ideas made thoroughly coherent by the principle of personalism. This principle argues that a life of generous self-giving to others in a personal way has greater social (and subjective) validity than a life filled with public acclaim, professed female liberationists to the contrary. The world of the family, in which the values of close personal association and child development become of supreme importance, is a world toward which many men gravitate as they grow older. In a somewhat subtler way there is a world of professional pride, according to which the achievement of excellence in one's occupation, be it secretary, priest, garage mechanic, or janitor, becomes a controlling principle of life. There is a world of the property-owner, who, having sacrificed for years to purchase what he now has, sees most public issues in the light of protection of his holding.

All of these worlds—those described at length earlier and those described here briefly—are or can become stable mentalities. They provide their inhabitants with fixed ideas that make life not only manageable, but also, because of the idealism that characterizes several of these worlds, positively satisfying. They become mental retreats, defended tentatively at first, then with intensity and emotion as one grows older.

# EPILOGUE

## THE AMERICAN SENSE OF ABSOLUTES

Whether because of national vanity or of national uncertainty, America is one of the most self-conscious nations on earth, willingly sitting for her portrait to be painted by all who would do so. Being a gracious and generous subject, she pays handsome fees for these portrayals, even when the image on the canvas is scarcely recognizable. The portraiture of America has been a major enterprise of American scholars in recent years, a more or less constant theme from them being that the aging lady has lost her innocence, and, indeed, her principles. America, it is said, has become a woman of the world, and sometimes of the streets. She is sadder, but wiser, a woman of flexibility and compromise. The trouble with this portrayal is that it is blurred by what some have called the irony of the artist: that a portrait is more often a reflection of the artist than of the sitter. In describing their country American intellectuals have all too often failed to depict the real America—grass-roots America—reporting instead their own preoccupations and those of their student associates. There are fertile reasons for their having done so.

Over the past century the American academic world has been

buffeted by wave after wave of relativistic thought systems. Whatever their specific names—positivism, pragmatism, existentialism, and others—each of them leaned to a naturalistic premise that there is no fixed ground of truth, nor any unchanging essence once called human nature. Rather there is only something called "the human condition." The implications of this philosophic nihilism were searchingly described by essayist Joseph Wood Krutch: "Take *tabula rasa* as a complete description of the brain with which a man is born and all the relativisms, moral, social, cultural, and aesthetic, logically follow. On a blank slate anything can be written." [1] Great numbers in the American academic world were swept along in the tidal current toward the "blank slate" theory and came to spend their energies in advocating freedom from traditional values of every kind—social, intellectual, moral. Their books bore the stamp of predominant commitment to identification of the new rather than to appraisal of continuity as modified by novel forms; their lectures manifested a lingering inference that values are inherently subjective rather than fixed or absolute. Thus emerged the "now mentality" described in an earlier chapter.

The bias toward present-mindedness brought by relativist views was deepened by other facets of academic life. Continuing cultural hostility toward intellectuals, or "eggheads" as they were sometimes called, made them resentful of traditional American mentality and disposed them hastily to report any seeming modification of the public mind. Day-to-day association with upper-middle-class urban collegians—the least tradition-minded of American youth—raised hopes that at last Americans were becoming "enlightened." Rapid technological innovations in industry and communications brought the conclusion—by parallelism —that the older mentality was changing at an equal pace. In addition to these forward forces there was the occupational tendency of the intellectual toward speculation, which sometimes functions to mix fancy and fact. The intellectual had little basis for understanding the grass-roots mind, and thus tended to read it according to his understandable bias. Finally, of further influence is the tendency—perhaps the emotional compulsion—of intellectuals, as a sociological species, to challenge the existing system and identify its failures according to abstract ideals. Such an orientation often leads to a sort of secular evangelism that closes one's mind to social realities.[2]

With academic perspectives thus shaped, the picture of the latter-day American often presented in histories and periodicals is that of one who has abandoned "traditional verities," or "familiar truths," or "the old morality," or "the faith of our fathers" in favor of "disquieting insecurities," or of "new perspectives appropriate to a modern age." It is the argument of this book that such descriptions are at best half-true and at worst a gross caricature of the American mind. They reflect too much attention to adolescents and young adults during their period of intellectual vagabondage, and too little attention to the majority of the population of twenty-five and older; [3] they reflect too much attention to the purely rational aspects of man and too little to the emotional and instinctive sides; they reflect too much attention to the principle of intelligence and too little to the principle of conservation of energy. In summary they reflect too much preoccupation with faddish ideas, youthful insecurity, and social adjustment, and too little awareness of the presence (and prescience) of traditional ideals, timeworn adages, and enlightened prejudices. Grass-roots Americans, for all of their limitations, retain a basic wisdom, best summarized by Samuel Johnson, who once said, "He is no wise man that will quit a certainty for an uncertainty."

But the view that has been presented in these pages is not that grass-roots Americans, collectively, are wise, though individually they well may be. The point argued here is that the grass-roots American mind has an essential stability that not only surmounts present crises, but also vibrates to most of the same rhythms that pulsed much earlier in American cultural life. Of course this is so. Is there not for all the same-as-always predilection for the concrete life, which, with its physical attractions, emotional magnets, and recurrent necessities, insulates one from (or numbs one to) both "logic" and a changing environment? Is there not that natural inertia that endlessly recommends retention of the old pattern that works? Are there not well-defined and ably defended retreats that make effective rejoinders to those who seek to impose the tyranny of the present? Is there not in popular culture, small-town culture, and ethnic culture a confirmation of values, sentiments, and prejudices that are somehow rational and emotionally comforting at the same time? Finally, is there not a basic human thirst for, and tendency toward, constancy, absolutes, the eternal, these leading to the development of bedrock principles? Indeed, given human and cultural patterns, it would be most surprising if major changes in public mentality occurred at anything more rapid than a glacial tempo.

One of the most fundamental divisions in American life is that between intellectuals and grass-roots Americans. They live in different worlds. The intellectual lives in a world of relativism and finds it manageable enough that he projects its lights upon his students. But in this other world the grass-roots American finds a different light, more diffuse and thus more versatile. He lives in a world of absolutes. The American sense of absolutes is fixed in the insights, intuitions, and inclinations of grass-roots America. By "sense of absolutes" is meant not a system of universals, nor a cluster of "infallible" truths, but a way of seeing life and a way of reacting to it that is stable, recurrent, and assured. The sense of absolutes is not entirely a matter of ultimate convictions, nor of fixed responses, nor of confident opinion, though from an individual standpoint it may be one or all of these. It is not a matter of social solidarity on certain given points; rather it is a case of fleeting constituencies on many different points. More than this, it is a basic orientation to life, a way of surviving the tendency to muddlement toward which all human affairs gravitate, and to which all human individuals are subject. With a "knowledge never learned of school," grass-roots Americans find their absolutes—some cultural and some personal—a basic survival kit in a framework of external change.

# NOTES

**CHAPTER ONE**

**1.** This and subsequent Will Rogers' quotes are taken from William R. Brown, *Imagemaker: Will Rogers and the American Dream* (Columbia, Mo.: University of Missouri Press, 1970), *passim.*

**2.** Eric Hoffer, *First Things, Last Things* (New York: Harper & Row, 1967, 1968, 1970, 1971), p. 75.

**3.** David Hackett Fischer, *Historians' Fallacies* (New York: Harper & Row, 1970), pp. 154–155.

**4.** Leland O. Baldwin, *The Stream of American History* (New York: American Book Company, 1952), p. 683.

**5.** R. W. B. Lewis, *The American Adam* (Chicago: University of Chicago Press, 1955), p. 4ff. Lewis' views are more fully discussed in Chapter Two in the section on American optimism.

**6.** Mark R. Hillegas, *The Future As Nightmare* (New York: Oxford University Press, 1967), p. 19ff.

**7.** Charles A. Reich, *The Greening of America* (New York: Random House, 1970), p. 393.

**8.** John Platt, *Perception and Change* (Ann Arbor, Mich.: University of Michigan Press, 1970), p. 120.

**9.** Ralph H. Gabriel, *American Values: Continuity and Change* (Westport, Conn.: Greenwood Press, 1974), p. 116.

**10.** P. M. Grady, rev. of *Future Shock,* by Alvin Toffler, *Book World,* September 6, 1970, p. 6.

**11.** J. H. Hexter, *The History Primer* (New York: Basic Books, 1971), p. 37.

**12.** Especially is this notable in *Time* and *Newsweek,* whose preoccupation with the latest news developments often further colors their writers' philosophical points of view toward reality.

**13.** Joseph Conrad, *Heart of Darkness* (New York: Bantam Books, 1960), p. 31.

**14.** Richard Hoggart, *The Uses of Literacy* (London: Chatto and Windus, 1957), p. 88. Hoggart's work as a whole provides many useful insights into the culture and style of common folk, these insights applicable beyond the English working class, which was the focus of his study.

**15.** *The New York Times,* March 17, 1976, 57, col. 6. Also cited in this article is a 1975 U.S. Office of Education study that found 22 percent of Americans over age 17 to be functional illiterates. An additional 32 percent were found to be marginal illiterates. Thus, 54 percent of the American population over 17 could be said to have serious reading comprehension problems. Also of interest in connection with the American literacy problem is the Comptroller General's Report to Congress *The Adult Basic Education Program: Progress in Reducing Illiteracy and Improvements Needed* (Washington, D.C.: GPO, 1975 [MWD-75-61]). The later observation that 50 percent of American newspaper readers cannot satisfactorily comprehend the front page is the judgment of Dr. Edward Fry, director of the Reading Institute at Rutgers University, as reported in *The Omaha World-Herald,* May 18, 1975, p. 1, col. 3.

## CHAPTER TWO

**1.** R. L. Bruckberger, *Image of America* (New York: Viking Press, 1959), p. 202.

**2.** Bernard Rosenberg, "Mass Culture in America," in *Mass Culture, The Popular Arts in America,* Bernard Rosenberg and David Manning White, editors (Glencoe, N.Y.: The Free Press, 1957), p. 7.

**3.** Susan Sontag, "One Culture and the New Sensibility," in *Popular Culture and the Expanding Consciousness,* Ray B. Browne, editor (New York: John Wiley & Sons, 1973), p. 28.

**4.** Roger B. Rollin, "Against Evaluation," *Journal of Popular Culture,* 9 (1975), pp. 361–363. See also Leslie A. Fiedler, "Toward a Definition of Popular Culture," in *Superculture* (Bowling Green, Ohio: Bowling Green University Popular Press, 1975), pp. 28–42.

**5.** John G. Cawelti, "The Concept of Formula in the Study of Popular Culture," *Journal of Popular Culture,* 3 (1969), p. 385.

**6.** Laurence Lerner, *The Uses of Nostalgia* (New York: Schocken Books, 1972), pp. 20–21.

**7.** Gary Topping, "Zane Grey's West," *Journal of Popular Culture,* 7 (1973), p. 681.

**8.** Orley I. Holtan, "The Agrarian Myth in *Midnight Cowboy, Alice's Restaurant, Easy Rider,* and *Medium Cool,*" *Journal of Popular Culture,* 4 (1970), pp. 273–286.

**9.** D. H. Lawrence, *Studies in Classic American Literature* (New York: Viking Press, 1964), p. 14ff.

**10.** John Tebbel, *From Rags to Riches* (New York: Macmillan, 1963), p. 12.

**11.** Arthur Prager, "Edward Stratemeyer and His Book Machine," *Saturday Review,* July 10, 1971. In this article Prager summarizes the main elements of the Stratemeyer story. A more general treatment of popular juvenile literature from 1910–1940 is provided in the same author's *Rascals at Large* (Garden City, N.Y.: Doubleday, 1971). For the sake of accuracy, it should be pointed out that Stratemeyer did not himself write every last word of every book. He "farmed out" themes and chapter outlines to hungry writers, but carefully edited their returned stories so that content and style remained consistent throughout each series. It was an assembly-line operation, partly anyway, but a carefully controlled one.

**12.** Prager, "Book Machine," *ibid.,* p. 15.

**13.** Prager, *Rascals at Large, ibid.,* p. 227.

**14.** Walter Evans, "The All-American Boys: A Study of Boys' Sports Fiction," *Journal of Popular Culture,* 6 (1972), pp. 104–105.

**15.** *Ibid.,* p. 115.

**16.** William D. Murray, *The History of the Boy Scouts* (New York: Boy Scouts of America, 1937), p. 200.

**17.** Will Oursler, *The Boy Scout Story* (Garden City, N.Y.: Doubleday, 1955), p. 126.

**18.** *Ibid.*, p. 70.

**19.** *Ibid.*, p. 16.

**20.** David Mead, "1914: The Chautauqua and American Innocence," *Journal of Popular Culture,* 1 (1968), p. 341.

**21.** Patrick Johns-Heine and Hans H. Gerth, "Values in Mass Periodical Fiction, 1921–40," *Public Opinion Quarterly,* Spring 1949, p. 113.

**22.** Bruce A. Lohof, "A Morphology of the Modern Fable," *Journal of Popular Culture,* 8 (1974), pp. 15–27.

**23.** David Sonenschein, "Love and Sex in the Romance Magazines," *Journal of Popular Culture,* 4 (1970), p. 406.

**24.** Statistics from Alice Payne Hackett, *70 Years of Best Sellers, 1895–1965* (New York: R. R. Bowker, 1967).

**25.** Ruth Suckow, "Hollywood Gods and Goddesses," *Harper's Magazine,* July 1936, p. 191.

**26.** Leo Gurko, *Heroes, Highbrows, and the Popular Mind* (Freeport, N.Y.: Books for Libraries Press, 1971), p. 193.

**27.** Norman L. Friedman, "American Movies and the American Culture, 1946–1970," *Journal of Popular Culture,* 3 (1970), p. 817.

**28.** Wolfgang Max Faust, "Comics and How to Read Them," *Journal of Popular Culture,* 5 (1971), p. 196.

**29.** Russell H. Weigel and Richard Jessor, "Television and Adolescent Conventionality: An Exploratory Study," *Public Opinion Quarterly,* 37 (1973), pp. 77–78. See also Thomas Stritch, "The Blurred Image: Some Reflections on the Mass Media in the 1960's," in *America in Change, Reflections on the 60's and 70's,* Ronald Weber, editor (Notre Dame, Ind.: University of Notre Dame Press, 1972), p. 219.

**30.** Pearl G. Aldrich, "Daniel Defoe: The Father of Soap Opera," *Journal of Popular Culture,* 8 (1975), p. 767. Ms. Aldrich here cites John J. Richetti, *Popular Fiction Before Richardson: Narrative Patterns 1700–1739,* p. 11.

**31.** Aldrich, *ibid.*, 770.

**32.** Kay J. Mussell, "Beautiful and Damned: The Sexual Woman in Gothic Fiction," *Journal of Popular Culture,* 9 (1975), p. 89.

**33.** Philippe Perebinossoff, "What Does a Kiss Mean? The Love Comic Formula and the Creation of the Ideal Teen-Age Girl," *Journal of Popular Culture,* 8 (1975), p. 834.

**34.** Nicholas M. Rinaldi, "The TV Savior Image: A Contemporary Myth," *Thought,* 41 (1966), pp. 229–230.

**35.** David W. Noble, *Historians Against History* (Minneapolis: University of Minnesota Press, 1965), p. 4ff.

**36.** See, for example, Eli Ginzberg, *The Optimistic Tradition and American Youth* (New York: Columbia University Press, 1962), p. 9ff.

**37.** John Bainbridge, *Little Wonder, or The Reader's Digest and How It Grew* (New York: Reynal & Hitchcock, 1945, 1946), p. 136.

**38.** Richard Schickel, *The Disney Version* (New York: Simon & Schuster, 1968), p. 19.

**39.** William McReynolds, "Walt Disney Plays the Glad Game," *Journal of Popular Culture,* 7 (1974), p. 795.

**40.** C. B. Spaulding, "Romantic Love Complex in American Culture," *Sociology and Social Research,* 55 (1970), p. 97.

**41.** S. I. Hayakawa, "Popular Songs vs. The Facts of Life," *Etc.,* 12 (1955), pp. 83–95.

**CHAPTER THREE**

**1.** U.S. Bureau of the Census, Census of Population: 1970, Vol. 1, *Characteristics of the Population,* Part 1, United States Summary, Section 1 (Washington, D.C.: U.S. Government Printing Office, 1973), pp. 1–43.

**2.** Cynthia Russ Ramsey, "Small Towns: Here I Can Leave a Footprint," in *Life in Rural America* (Washington, D.C.: National Geographic Society, 1974), p. 61.

**3.** See Edward Margolies, "City, Nature, Highway: Changing Images in American Film and Theater," *Journal of Popular Culture,* 9 (1975), pp. 14–19.

**4.** Karl Menninger, M.D., *A Psychiatrist's World* (New York: Viking Press, 1959), p. 30.

**5.** Calvin L. Beale, "The Revival of Population Growth in Nonmetropolitan America," Economic Development Division, Economic Research Service, U.S. Department of Agriculture, ERS-605, Item 42-I. Beale's article is a commentary on the Census Bureau's December 1974 report. He points out that during the 1960s there was an average yearly "outmovement" from rural areas of 300,000 people per year;

during the 1970s—so far—there has been an average yearly "inmovement" to rural areas of 353,000. Nor is this at all traceable to "urban sprawl," since counties nonadjacent to urban areas have grown rapidly. Beale concludes that we have reached the end of the "unchallenged validity" of continued urban concentration.

**6.** Robert C. Wood, *Suburbia, Its People and Their Politics* (Boston: Houghton Mifflin, 1958), p. 260.

**7.** Robert Nisbet, *Twilight of Authority* (New York: Oxford University Press, 1975), p. 261.

**8.** Granville Hicks, *Small Town* (New York: Macmillan, 1947), p. 218.

**9.** Peter Schrag, "Is Main Street Still There," *Saturday Review,* January 17, 1970, p. 25.

**9a.** Benjamin Stein, "Whatever Happened to Small-Town America?" *The Public Interest,* 44 (1976), p. 20ff.

**10.** Bill Cole, interview with F. Gerald Kline (editor of the *Journal of Communication Research*), St. Louis *Globe-Democrat,* March 13–14, 1976, p. 3B, cols. 7 and 8.

**11.** Bradford Smith, *Why We Behave Like Americans* (Philadelphia: J. B. Lippincott, 1957), p. 101.

**12.** Albert Blumenthal, *Small-Town Stuff* (Chicago: University of Chicago Press, 1932), p. 110.

**13.** Zona Gale, *Friendship Village Love Stories* (New York: Macmillan, 1909), p. 6.

**14.** Hicks, *op. cit.,* p. 102.

**15.** Joseph P. Lyford, *The Talk in Vandalia* (Santa Barbara, Calif.: The Fund for the Republic, 1962), p. 101.

**16.** James West, *Plainville, U.S.A.* (New York: Columbia University Press, 1945), p. 69.

**17.** Arthur J. Vidich and Joseph Bensman, *Small Town in Mass Society* (Princeton, N.J.: Princeton University Press, 1958), p. 44.

**18.** Lyford, *op. cit.,* p. 33.

**19.** Newell Leroy Sims, *Hoosier Village* (New York: Longmans, Green, 1912), p. 54.

**20.** Olney Sweet, "An Iowa County Seat," *Iowa Journal of History,* 38 (1940), p. 343.

**21.** Arnold Rose, "Anti-Semitism's Roots in City Hatred," *Commentary,* October 1948, p. 376.

**22.** Hicks, *op. cit.*, p. 141.

**23.** Page Smith, *As a City Upon a Hill; The Town in American History* (New York: Alfred A. Knopf, 1971), p. 83.

**24.** Hicks, *op. cit.*, p. 156.

**25.** Smith, *op. cit.*, p. 283.

**26.** William Faulkner, *Absalom, Absalom!* (New York: Random House, 1936), p. 361.

**27.** John Shelton Reed, *The Enduring South* (Chapel Hill, N.C.: University of North Carolina Press, 1974), p. 83ff.

**28.** Robert Frost, "The Gift Outright," in *Complete Poems of Robert Frost* (New York: Holt, Rinehart and Winston, 1967), p. 467.

**29.** W. J. Cash, *The Mind of the South* (New York: Alfred A. Knopf, 1941), p. 46.

**30.** James McBride Dabbs, *The Southern Heritage* (New York: Alfred A. Knopf, 1959), p. 28.

**31.** David M. Potter, "The Enigma of the South," *The Yale Review,* 51 (1961), pp. 150–151.

**32.** Cash, *op. cit.*, p. 31.

**33.** Dabbs, *op. cit.*, p. 169.

**34.** Daniel J. Elazar, *American Federalism, A View From the States* (New York: Thomas Y. Crowell, 1972), p. 103ff.

**35.** C. Vann Woodward, *The Burden of Southern History* (Baton Rouge, La.: Louisiana State University Press, 1968), p. 189.

**36.** Cash, *op. cit.*, p. 104.

## CHAPTER FOUR

**1.** Henrik Ibsen, "Ghosts," in *The Collected Works of Henrik Ibsen,* Vol. VII (New York: Charles Scribner's Sons, 1908), p. 225.

**2.** Cited in Stephen Bonsal, *Unfinished Business* (Garden City, N.Y.: Doubleday, Doran, 1944), pp. 68–69.

**3.** Jacques Barzun, *Classic, Romantic and Modern* (Boston: Little, Brown, 1943, 1961), p. 15.

**4.** Robert H. Wiebe, *The Segmented Society* (New York: Oxford University Press, 1975), p. 24ff.

**5.** Robert K. Merton, *Social Theory and Social Structure* (Glencoe, N.Y.: The Free Press, 1957), p. 126.

**6.** Lewis A. Coser, *Greedy Institutions* (New York: The Free Press, 1974), p. 4.

**7.** U.S. Bureau of the Census, 1970, Vol. 1, Part 1, *Characteristics of the Population,* Section 2, p. 718ff.

**8.** R. Joseph Monsen, "The American Business View," *Daedalus,* 98 (1969), p. 159–173. Monsen's classification is extremely broad, but appropriate to the present purpose.

**9.** All statistics used here were taken from *Dun's Market Identifiers,* bearing a date of January 1, 1975. Data was furnished by Dun & Bradstreet, Marketing Services Division, Home Office, 99 Church Street, New York, N.Y. 10007. The statistics used here are very conservative so far as the number of small businesses is concerned. Not included, for example, are such businesses as architectural firms and barbershops.

**10.** John H. Bunzel, *The American Small Businessman* (New York: Alfred A. Knopf, 1962), p. 125.

**11.** *Ibid.,* p. 89ff.

**12.** Neil W. Chamberlain, "The Life of the Mind in the Firm," *Daedalus,* 98 (1969), p. 136.

**13.** Robert Presthus, *The Organizational Society* (New York: Vintage Books, 1962), p. 7ff.

**14.** William H. Whyte, Jr., *The Organization Man* (New York: Simon & Schuster, 1956), p. 3.

**15.** See Richard M. Huber, *The American Idea of Success* (New York: McGraw-Hill, 1971), p. 251ff.

**16.** Rudyard Kipling, "Tommy," in *Ballads and Barrack Room Ballads,* 1892, 1893.

**17.** All statistics taken from *U.S. Bureau of the Census, Statistical Abstract of the United States,* 1974 (Washington, D.C.: U.S. Government Printing Office, 1974), pp. 315–325.

**18.** Charles H. Coates and Roland J. Pellegrin, *Military Sociology* (University Park, Md.: Social Science Press, 1965), p. 374.

**19.** Robert A. Nisbet, "The Coming Problem of Assimilation," *The American Journal of Sociology,* 50 (1945), pp. 264–265.

**20.** Alfred Schuetz, "The Stranger: An Essay in Social Psychology," *The American Journal of Sociology,* 49 (1944), pp. 499–507.

**21.** Morris Janowitz, *The Professional Soldier* (Glencoe, N.Y.: The Free Press, 1960), p. 189.

**22.** Charles C. Moskos, Jr., *The American Enlisted Man* (New York: Russell Sage Foundation, 1970), p. 62.

**23.** *Ibid.*, p. 71.

**24.** Howard Brotz and Everett Wilson, "Characteristics of Military Society," *The American Journal of Sociology,* 51 (1946), p. 371.

**25.** Milton Rokeach, "Faith, Hope and Bigotry," *Psychology Today,* April 1970, p. 58.

**26.** See Clifford Geertz, "Ideology as a Cultural System," in *Ideology and Discontent,* David E. Apter, editor (New York: The Free Press, 1964), p. 47ff.

**27.** *Yearbook of American and Canadian Churches, 1975,* Constant H. Jacquet, Jr., editor (Nashville, Tenn., and New York: Abingdon Press, 1975), pp. 262–263.

**28.** See Douglas T. Miller, "Popular Religion of the 1950's," *Journal of Popular Culture,* 9 (1975), p. 68ff.

**29.** James Hitchcock, *The Decline and Fall of Radical Catholicism* (New York: Herder and Herder, 1971), p. 45ff.

**30.** Andrew Greeley, *Catholic Schools in a Declining Church* (New York: Sheed & Ward, 1976).

**31.** "Why Catholic Churchmen Worry About the Future," *U.S. News & World Report,* May 20, 1974, pp. 31–32.

**32.** Michael Parenti, "Political Values and Religious Cultures: Jews, Catholics and Protestants," *Journal for the Scientific Study of Religion,* 6 (1967), p. 264.

**33.** *Ibid.*, p. 263.

**34.** R. L. Bruckberger, "The American Catholics as a Minority," in *Roman Catholicism in Twentieth Century America,* Thomas T. McAvoy, editor (Notre Dame, Ind.: University of Notre Dame Press, 1960), p. 46.

**35.** Seymour Martin Lipset, *The First New Nation* (Garden City, N.Y.: Doubleday, 1963), p. 173.

**36.** Parenti, *op. cit.*, 266.

**37.** Specifically included here as being in the fundamentalist camp are southern Baptists, Missouri Synod Lutherans, some American Baptists, and a number of the "sects," including, among others, Churches of God, Assemblies of God, Adventists, and some Pentecostal churches. Further, there are strongly conservative components of the Wesleyan Methodist Church and the Orthodox Presbyterian Church.

**38.** Walter H. Clark, *The Psychology of Religion* (New York: Macmillan, 1958), p. 220ff.

**39.** Wallace Turner, *The Mormon Establishment* (Boston: Houghton Mifflin, 1966), p. 291.

**40.** William Gellerman, *The American Legion as Educator* (New York: Bureau of Publications, Teachers College, Columbia University, 1938). See especially p. 264ff.

**41.** Raymond Moley, Jr., *The American Legion Story* (New York: Meredith, 1966), p. 141.

**42.** Robert N. Bellah, "Civil Religion in America," *Daedalus* 96 (1967), pp. 1–21.

**43.** See David M. Potter, "American Individualism in the Twentieth Century," in *Innocence and Power,* Gordon Mills, editor (Austin: University of Texas Press, 1965).

**44.** Will Herberg, *Protestant-Catholic-Jew* (Garden City, N.Y.: Doubleday, 1955), pp. 88–89.

**45.** See Edward M. Burns, *The American Idea of Mission* (New Brunswick, N.J.: Rutgers University Press, 1957); Russel B. Nye, *This Almost Chosen People* (East Lansing, Mich.: Michigan State University Press, 1966); and Conrad Cherry, *God's New Israel* (Englewood Cliffs, N.J.: Prentice-Hall, 1971).

**46.** U.S. Bureau of the Census, Vol. 1, Part 1, Sections 1 and 2, *Characteristics of the Population,* p. 598.

**47.** Perry L. Weed, *The White Ethnic Movement and Ethnic Politics* (New York: Praeger, 1973), pp. 4–5.

**48.** Michael Parenti, "Ethnic Politics and the Persistence of Ethnic Identification," *The American Political Science Review* 61 (1967), p. 719.

**49.** Parenti, "Ethnic Politics," *op. cit.,* p. 723.

**50.** See Andrew M. Greeley, *Why Can't They Be More Like Us* (New York: E. P. Dutton, 1971), p. 95ff.

**51.** Cited by Michael Novak, *The Rise of the Unmeltable Ethnics* (New York: Macmillan, 1971, 1972), p. 33.

**52.** Parenti, "Ethnic Politics," *op. cit.,* p. 719.

**53.** Novak, *op. cit.,* 211–212.

**54.** Novak, *op. cit.,* 48.

**55.** Richard Lemon, *The Troubled American* (New York: Simon & Schuster, 1969, 1970), p. 109.

## EPILOGUE

**1.** Joseph Wood Krutch, *Human Nature and the Human Condition* (New York: Random House, 1959), p. 165–66.

**2.** See Lewis S. Feuer, *Ideology and the Ideologists* (New York: Harper & Row, 1975), p. 204ff.

**3.** According to the most recent census figures (1974), exactly 20.6 percent of the population are in the 14–24 age range, 55.6 percent of the population are 25 and older, and of these fully 41.6 percent are over 35. U.S. Bureau of the Census, *Statistical Abstract of the United States,* 1975, p. 31.

# BIBLIOGRAPHY

Aldrich, Pearl G. "Daniel Defoe: The Father of Soap Opera." *Journal of Popular Culture,* 8 (1975), p. 767.

Anderson, Sherwood. *Perhaps Women.* New York: Horace Liveright, 1931.

Atherton, Lewis. *Main Street on the Middle Border.* Chicago: Quadrangle Books, 1966.

Bainbridge, John. *Little Wonder, or The Reader's Digest and How It Grew.* New York: Reynal & Hitchcock, 1945, 1946.

Baldwin, Leland O. *The Stream of American History,* Volume 1. New York: American Book Company, 1952.

Barzun, Jacques. *Classic, Romantic and Modern.* Boston: Little, Brown, 1943, 1961.

Beale, Calvin L. "The Revival of Population Growth in Nonmetropolitan America." Economic Development Division, Economic Research Service, U.S. Department of Agriculture. ERS-605, Item 42-I, pp. 3–15.

Bellah, Robert N. "Civil Religion in America." *Daedalus* 96 (1967), pp. 1–21.

Blumenthal, Albert. *Small-Town Stuff*. Chicago: University of Chicago Press, 1932.

Bonsal, Stephen. *Unfinished Business*. Garden City, N.Y.: Doubleday, Doran, 1944.

Booth, Edward Townsend. *God Made the Country*. New York: Alfred A. Knopf, 1946.

Boulding, Kenneth E. *The Meaning of the Twentieth Century*. New York: Harper & Row, 1964.

Brooks, Van Wyck. *America's Coming of Age*. Garden City, N.Y.: Doubleday Anchor Books, 1958.

Brotz, Howard, and Wilson, Everett. "Characteristics of Military Society." *The American Journal of Sociology,* 51 (1946), p. 371.

Brown, William R. *Imagemaker: Will Rogers and the American Dream*. Columbia, Mo.: University of Missouri Press, 1970.

Bruckberger, R. L. *Image of America*. New York: Viking Press, 1959.
————. "The American Catholics as a Minority." *Roman Catholicism in Twentieth Century America*. Thomas T. McAvoy, editor. Notre Dame, Ind.: University of Notre Dame Press, 1960, p. 46.

Bruner, Jerome. *The Process of Education*. Cambridge, Mass.: Harvard University Press, 1960.

Buckler, Helen, *et al. Wo-He-Lo, The Story of the Camp Fire Girls, 1910–1960*. New York: Holt, Rinehart, and Winston, 1961.

Bunzel, John H. *The American Small Businessman*. New York: Alfred A. Knopf, 1962.

Burns, Edward M. *The American Idea of Mission*. New Brunswick, N.J.: Rutgers University Press, 1957.

Cash, W. J. *The Mind of the South*. New York: Alfred A. Knopf, 1941.

Cawelti, John G. "The Concept of Formula in the Study of Popular Culture." *Journal of Popular Culture,* 3 (1969), p. 385.

Chamberlain, Neil W. "The Life of the Mind in the Firm." *Daedalus,* 98 (1969), p. 136.

Cherry, Conrad. *God's New Israel*. Englewood Cliffs, N.J.: Prentice-Hall, 1971.

Chesterton, G. K. *Chaucer*. London: Faber & Faber Limited, 1932.

Clark, Walter H. *The Psychology of Religion*. New York: Macmillan, 1958.

Coates, Charles, and Pellegrin, Roland J. *Military Sociology*. University Park, Md.: Social Science Press, 1965.

Cole, Bill. Interview with F. Gerald Kline. St. Louis *Globe-Democrat*, March 13–14, 1976, p. 3B.

Conrad, Joseph. *Heart of Darkness*. New York: Bantam Books, 1960.

Coser, Lewis A. *Greedy Institutions*. New York: The Free Press, 1974.

Dabbs, James McBride. *The Southern Heritage*. New York: Alfred A. Knopf, 1959.

Donovan, James A. *Militarism, U.S.A.* New York: Charles Scribner's Sons, 1970.

Dreiser, Theodore. *Hey-Rub-A-Dub-Dub*. New York: Boni and Liveright, 1920.

*Dun's Market Identifiers,* January 1, 1975. Dun & Bradstreet, Marketing Services Division, New York.

Elazar, Daniel J. *American Federalism, A View From the States*. New York: Thomas Y. Crowell, 1972.

*Encyclopedia Americana,* International Edition. New York: Americana Corporation, 1973.

Evans, Walter. "The All-American Boys: A Study of Boys' Sports Fiction." *Journal of Popular Culture,* 6 (1972), pp. 104–105.

Farrell, James T. *The League of Frightened Philistines*. New York: Vanguard Press, 1945.

Faulkner, William. *Absalom, Absalom!* New York: Random House, 1936.

Faust, Wolfgang Max. "Comics and How to Read Them." *Journal of Popular Culture,* 5 (1971), p. 196.

Feuer, Lewis S. *Ideology and the Ideologists*. New York: Harper & Row, 1975.

Fiedler, Leslie A. "Toward a Definition of Popular Literature." *Superculture*. Bowling Green, Ohio: Bowling Green University Popular Press, 1975.

Fischer, David Hackett. *Historians' Fallacies*. New York: Harper & Row, 1970.

Friedman, Norman L. "American Movies and the American Culture, 1946–1970." *Journal of Popular Culture,* 3 (1970), p. 817.

Frost, Robert. "The Gift Outright." *Complete Poems of Robert Frost*. New York: Holt, Rinehart, and Winston, 1967.

*The Futurist.* Washington, D.C.: World Future Society, 7 (1973).

Gabriel, Ralph H. *American Values: Continuity and Change.* Westport, Conn.: Greenwood Press, 1974.

Gale, Zona. *Friendship Village Love Stories.* New York: Macmillan, 1909.

Gans, Herbert J. *The Urban Villagers.* Glencoe, N.Y.: The Free Press, 1962.

Gardner, John W. *Self-Renewal.* New York: Harper & Row, 1963.

Geertz, Clifford. "Ideology as a Cultural System." *Ideology and Discontent.* David E. Apter, editor. New York: The Free Press, 1964.

Gellerman, William. *The American Legion as Educator.* New York: Bureau of Publications, Teachers College, Columbia University, 1938.

Ginzberg, Eli. *The Optimistic Tradition and American Youth.* New York: Columbia University Press, 1962.

Grady, P. M. *Book World,* September 6, 1970, p. 6.

Greeley, Andrew M. *Catholic Schools in a Declining Church.* New York: Sheed & Ward, 1976.

————. *Why Can't They Be More Like Us.* New York: E. P. Dutton, 1971.

Gurko, Leo. *Heroes, Highbrows, and the Popular Mind.* Freeport, N.Y.: Books for Libraries Press, 1971.

Hackett, Alice Payne. *70 Years of Best Sellers, 1895–1965.* New York: R. R. Bowker, 1967.

Halsey, Margaret. *The Pseudo-Ethic.* New York: Simon & Schuster, 1963.

Harrold, Charles Frederick, ed. *A Newman Treasury.* New York: Longmans, Green, 1943.

Hasbany, Richard. "Bromidic Parables: The American Musical Theatre During the Second World War." *Journal of Popular Culture,* 6 (1973), pp. 642–665.

Hayakawa, S. I. "Popular Songs vs. The Facts of Life." *Etc.,* 12 (1955), pp. 83–95.

Heilbroner, Robert J. *The Future as History.* New York: Harper & Row, 1959, 1960.

Herberg, Will. *Protestant-Catholic-Jew.* Garden City, N.Y.: Doubleday, 1955.

Hexter, J. H. *The History Primer,* New York: Basic Books, 1971.

Hicks, Granville. *Small Town*. New York: Macmillan, 1947.

Hillegas, Mark R. *The Future as Nightmare*. New York: Oxford University Press, 1967.

Hitchcock, James. *The Decline and Fall of Radical Catholicism*. New York: Herder and Herder, 1971.

Hoffer, Eric. *First Things, Last Things*. New York: Harper & Row, 1967, 1968, 1970, 1971.

Hofstadter, Richard. *Anti-Intellectualism in American Life*. New York: Alfred A. Knopf, 1963.

Hoggart, Richard. *The Uses of Literacy*. London: Chatto and Windus, 1957.

Holtan, Orley I. "The Agrarian Myth in *Midnight Cowboy, Alice's Restaurant, Easy Rider,* and *Medium Cool*." *Journal of Popular Culture*, 4 (1970), pp. 273–286.

Huber, Richard M. *The American Idea of Success*. New York: McGraw-Hill, 1971.

Ibsen, Henrik. "Ghosts." *The Collected Works of Henrik Ibsen,* Vol. 7. New York: Charles Scribner's Sons, 1908.

Janowitz, Morris. *The Professional Soldier*. Glencoe, N.Y.: The Free Press, 1960.

Johns-Heine, Patrick, and Gerth, Hans H. "Values in Mass Periodical Fiction, 1921–40." *Public Opinion Quarterly,* 12 (1949), p. 113.

Kipling, Rudyard. "Tommy." *Ballads and Barrack Room Ballads*. 1892, 1893.

Krutch, Joseph Wood. *Human Nature and the Human Condition*. New York: Random House, 1959.

Landis, Paul H. *Rural Life in Process*. New York: McGraw-Hill, 1948.

Lawrence, D. H. *Studies in Classic American Literature*. New York: Viking Press, 1964.

Lemon, Richard. *The Troubled American*. New York: Simon & Schuster, 1969, 1970.

Lerner, Laurence. *The Uses of Nostalgia*. New York: Schocken Books, 1972.

Lewis, R. W. B. *The American Adam, Innocence, Tragedy, and Tradition in the Nineteenth Century*. Chicago: University of Chicago Press, 1955.

Lipset, Seymour Martin. *The First New Nation*. Garden City, N.Y.: Doubleday, 1963.

Lohof, Bruce A. "A Morphology of the Modern Fable." *Journal of Popular Culture,* 8 (1974), pp. 15–27.

Lyford, Joseph P. *The Talk in Vandalia.* Santa Barbara, Calif.: The Fund for the Republic, 1962.

Maddox, John. *The Doomsday Syndrome.* New York: McGraw-Hill, 1972.

Margolies, Edward. "City, Nature, Highway: Changing Images in American Film and Theater." *Journal of Popular Culture,* 9 (1975), pp. 14–19.

McPherson, William. *Ideology and Change: Radicalism and Fundamentalism in America.* Palo Alto, Calif.: National Press Books, 1973.

McReynolds, William. "Walt Disney Plays the Glad Game." *Journal of Popular Culture,* 7 (1974), p. 795.

Mead, David. "1914: The Chautauqua and American Innocence." *Journal of Popular Culture,* 1 (1968), p. 341.

Mencken, H. L. *Notes on Democracy.* New York: Alfred A. Knopf, 1926.

Menninger, Karl. *A Psychiatrist's World.* New York: Viking Press, 1959.

Merton, Robert K. *Social Theory and Social Structure.* Glencoe, N.Y.: The Free Press, 1957.

Miller, Douglas T. "Popular Religion of the 1950's." *Journal of Popular Culture,* 9 (1975), p. 68.

Mills, C. Wright. *White Collar.* New York: Oxford University Press, 1951.

Moley, Raymond, Jr. *The American Legion Story.* New York: Meredith, 1966.

Monsen, R. Joseph. "The American Business View." *Daedalus,* 98 (1969), pp. 159–173.

Moskos, Charles C., Jr. *The American Enlisted Man.* New York: Russell Sage Foundation, 1970.

Mowry, George E. *The Urban Nation, 1920–1960.* New York: Hill & Wang, 1965.

Murray, William D. *The History of the Boy Scouts.* New York: Boy Scouts of America, 1937.

Mussell, Kay J. "Beautiful and Damned: The Sexual Woman in Gothic Fiction." *Journal of Popular Culture,* 9 (1975), p. 89.

*The New York Times,* January 6, June 29, July 24, 26, and 31, and August 2, 1914.

Nisbet, Robert A. "The Coming Problem of Assimilation." *The American Journal of Sociology,* 50 (1945), pp. 264–265.

———. *Twilight of Authority.* New York: Oxford University Press, 1975.

Noble, David W. *Historians Against History.* Minneapolis: University of Minnesota Press, 1965.

Novak, Michael. *The Rise of the Unmeltable Ethnics.* New York: Macmillan, 1971, 1972.

Nye, Russel B. *The Unembarrassed Muse, The Popular Arts in America.* New York: Dial Press, 1970.

———. *This Almost Chosen People.* East Lansing, Mich.: Michigan State University Press, 1966.

*Omaha World-Herald,* May 18, 1975.

Oursler, Will. *The Boy Scout Story.* Garden City, N.Y.: Doubleday, 1955.

Parenti, Michael. "Ethnic Politics and the Persistence of Ethnic Identification." *The American Political Science Review,* 61 (1967), p. 719.

———. "Political Values and Religious Cultures: Jews, Catholics and Protestants." *Journal for the Scientific Study of Religion,* 6 (1967), pp. 263–266.

Perebinossoff, Philippe. "What Does a Kiss Mean? The Love Comic Formula and the Creation of the Ideal Teen-Age Girl." *Journal of Popular Culture,* 8 (1975), p. 834.

Platt, John. *Perception and Change.* Ann Arbor, Mich.: University of Michigan Press, 1970.

"Population Estimates and Projections," U.S. Department of Commerce, Bureau of the Census, Series P-35, No. 537, issued December 1974.

Potter, David M. "American Individualism in the Twentieth Century." *Innocence and Power.* Gordon Mills, editor. Austin: University of Texas Press, 1965.

———. "The Enigma of the South." *The Yale Review,* 51 (1961), pp. 150–151.

Prager, Arthur. "Edward Stratemeyer and His Book Machine." *Saturday Review,* July 10, 1971.

————. *Rascals at Large.* Garden City, N. Y.: Doubleday, 1971.

Presthus, Robert. *The Organizational Society.* New York: Vintage Books, 1962.

Ramsey, Cynthia Russ. "Small Towns: Here I Can Leave a Footprint." *Life in Rural America.* Washington, D.C.: National Geographic Society, 1974.

Reed, John Shelton. *The Enduring South.* Chapel Hill, N.C.: University of North Carolina Press, 1974.

Reich, Charles A. *The Greening of America.* New York: Random House, 1970.

Richey, Russell E., and Jones, Donald G. *American Civil Religion.* New York: Harper & Row, 1974.

Rinaldi, Nicholas M. "The TV Savior Image: A Contemporary Myth." *Thought,* 41 (1966), pp. 229–230.

Rokeach, Milton. "Faith, Hope and Bigotry." *Psychology Today,* April 1970, p. 58.

Rollin, Roger B. "Against Evaluation." *Journal of Popular Culture,* 9 (1975), pp. 361–363.

Rose, Arnold. "Anti-Semitism's Roots in City Hatred." *Commentary,* October 1948, p. 376.

Rosenberg, Bernard, and White, David Manning. *Mass Culture, The Popular Arts in America.* Glencoe, N.Y.: The Free Press, 1957.

Salisbury, W. Seward. *Religion in American Culture.* Homewood, Ill.: Dorsey Press, 1964.

Schickel, Richard. *The Disney Version.* New York: Simon & Schuster, 1968.

Schrag, Peter. "Is Main Street Still There?" *Saturday Review,* January 17, 1970, p. 25.

Schuetz, Alfred. "The Stranger: An Essay in Social Psychology." *The American Journal of Sociology,* 49 (1944), pp. 499–507.

Sexton, Patricia Cayo, and Sexton, Brendan. *Blue Collars and Hard Hats.* New York: Random House, 1971.

Sims, Newell Leroy. *Hoosier Village.* New York: Longmans, Green, 1912.

Smith, Bradford. *Why We Behave Like Americans.* Philadelphia: J. B. Lippincott, 1957.

Smith, Page. *As a City Upon a Hill: The Town in American History.* New York: Alfred A. Knopf, 1971.

Sonenschein, David. "Love and Sex in the Romance Magazines." *Journal of Popular Culture,* 4 (1970), p. 406.

Sontag, Susan. "One Culture and the New Sensibility." *Popular Culture and the Expanding Consciousness.* Ray B. Browne, editor. New York: John Wiley & Sons, 1973.

Spaulding, C. B. "Romantic Love Complex in American Culture." *Sociology and Social Research,* 55 (1970), p. 97.

Stedman, Raymond W. *The Serials.* Norman, Okla.: University of Oklahoma Press, 1971.

Stein, Benjamin. "Whatever Happened to Small-Town America?" *The Public Interest,* 44 (1976), p. 20ff.

Streiker, Lowell D., and Strober, Gerald. *Religion and the New Majority.* New York: Association Press, 1972.

Suckow, Ruth. "Hollywood Gods and Goddesses." *Harper's Magazine,* July 1936, p. 191.

Sweet, Olney. "An Iowa County Seat." *Iowa Journal of History,* 38 (1940), p. 343.

Tebbel, John. *From Rags to Riches.* New York: Macmillan, 1963.

Tholfsen, Trygve R. *Historical Thinking.* New York: Harper & Row, 1967.

Topping, Gary. "Zane Grey's West." *Journal of Popular Culture,* 7 (1973), p. 681.

Turner, Wallace. *The Mormon Establishment.* Boston: Houghton Mifflin, 1966.

U.S. Bureau of the Census, Census of Population: 1970, Vol. 1, *Characteristics of the Population,* Part 1, United States Summary, Sections 1 and 2. Washington, D.C.: U.S. Government Printing Office, 1973.

U.S. Bureau of the Census, *Statistical Abstract of the United States.* Washington, D.C.: U.S. Government Printing Office, 1974, 1975.

Vidich, Arthur J., and Bensman, Joseph. *Small Town in Mass Society.* Princeton, N.J.: Princeton University Press, 1958.

Walsh, Warren B. *Perspectives and Patterns: Discourses on History.* Syracuse, N.Y.: Syracuse University Press, 1962.

Weber, Ronald, ed. *America in Change, Reflections on the 60's and 70's.* Notre Dame, Ind.: University of Notre Dame Press, 1972.

Weed, Perry L. *The White Ethnic Movement and Ethnic Politics.* New York: Praeger, 1973.

Weigel, Russell H., and Jessor, Richard. "Television and Adolescent Conventionality: An Exploratory Study." *Public Opinion Quarterly,* 37 (1973), pp. 77–78.

West, James. *Plainville, U.S.A.* New York: Columbia University Press, 1945.

"Why Catholic Churchmen Worry About the Future." *U.S. News & World Report,* May 20, 1974, pp. 31–32.

Whyte, William H., Jr. *The Organization Man.* New York: Simon & Schuster, 1956.

Wiebe, Robert H. *The Segmented Society.* New York: Oxford University Press, 1975.

Wilson, Charles M. *Backwoods America.* Chapel Hill, N.C.: University of North Carolina Press, 1935.

Wood, James Playsted. *Magazines in the United States.* New York: Ronald Press, 1956.

Wood, Robert C. *Suburbia, Its People and Their Politics.* Boston: Houghton Mifflin, 1958.

Woodward, C. Vann. *The Burden of Southern History.* Baton Rouge, La.: Louisiana State University Press, 1968.

*The World Almanac, 1975.* New York: Newspaper Enterprise Association, Inc., 1974.

*Yearbook of American and Canadian Churches, 1975.* Constant H. Jacquet, Jr., editor. Nashville, Tenn., and New York: Abingdon Press, 1975.

Young, William H., Jr. "The Serious Funnies: Adventure Comics During the Depression, 1929–1938." *Journal of Popular Culture,* 3 (1969), pp. 404–427.

# INDEX

# ABOUT THE AUTHOR

Conal Furay is professor of history at Webster College, St. Louis. He was educated at Creighton University, Omaha (M.A.) and St. Louis University (Ph.D.).